THE RAGGED PROMISED LAND:
JACK KEROUAC'S AMERICA
AND OTHER SCENES

The ragged promised land: Jack Kerouac's America and other scenes

GREGORY STEPHENSON

Ober-Limbo Verlag

Grateful acknowledgement is made to the editors of *Eclectica* and *Empty Mirror,* in which several essays and reviews in this volume have previously appeared.

Published by Ober-Limbo Verlag
Heidelberg, Germany

ISBN 978-87-971569-2-6

Cover design & layout by Birgit Stephenson

For Birgit

“You’re a genius
all the time.”

CONTENTS

The Ragged Promised Land:
Jack Kerouac's America / page 9

Poetic License: Gregory Corso
as a Young Felon / page 73

Before and After Desolation:
Kerouac at the Hotel Stevens / page 92

Mutinous Jester: Akbar del Piombo's
Collage Novels / page 103

"Curious and not Un-Poetical":
An anon. Cannabis Writing / page 122

A Few Far-Flung Fragments
of Forgotten Kerouaciana / page 132

Wounds of Wonder:
Samuel Greenberg / page 142

On the Dangerous Edge:
Jerry Kamstra / page 150

THE RAGGED PROMISED LAND: JACK KEROUAC'S AMERICA

"the ragged promised land …
old tumbledown holy America"
On the Road

There is a sense in which the entire canon of Jack Kerouac's works can be understood as a record of the author's attempts to fix a position for himself both in relation to eternity and to the temporal world. At the center of his writing is a hero (most often an alter-ego) who strives to align his life with the Absolute and to orient himself aright – according to his own lights – within the country and the culture into which he was born. It is this latter aspect of the Kerouac quest – the endeavours on the part of the author and his fictional protagonists to find meaningful engagement with the principles and institutions, customs and conventions that make up the social environment of the United States – this essay proposes to examine. My aim is to inquire into the author's response to and reflections upon the people and places of his native land as they are expressed in his novels, essays and other writings. To this end, I will consider the ways in which in these same writings Kerouac describes and interprets the America he meets, and attempt to illuminate the values and meanings that he finds there or finds to be absent. My approach to the topic will be roughly but not strictly chronological (based occasionally upon affinities or tensions, overlaps and contrasts between certain works) and although reasonably broad-based within Kerouac's body of writing will not be comprehensive.

In regard to my intention of tracing through the many pages of the author's work the shape of Kerouac's "Visions of America" (as he named them in an untitled poem) mention of what is commonly called "the American Dream" is inevitable.[1]

Scholars have, however, pointed to the profound ambiguity of the phrase. Lawrence R. Samuel remarks that the term is "mutable and amorphous ...it could mean whatever we want or need it to mean ... accommodating virtually any preconception or agenda." [2] In his history of the American Dream, Jim Cullen concurs: "... there is no *one* American Dream. Instead, there are many American *Dreams.*" [3] Similarly, Frederick Ives Carpenter states that "The American Dream has never been defined exactly, and probably never can be. It is both too various and too vague; many men have meant many different things by it." [4] Likewise, Jennifer L. Hochschild observes that "the idea of the American dream has been attached to everything from religious freedom to a home in the suburbs." [5] Robert H. Fossum and John K. Roth sum up neatly and succinctly, I think, the elusive nature of the concept of the American Dream: "Few terms are defined in so many different ways or bandied about more loosely than 'the American Dream' ... the Dream is and always has been comprised of many dreams; no single vision has ever totally dominated the American imagination." [6]

Notwithstanding widespread imprecise, reductive and indiscriminate applications of the phrase, certain core components of what is called the American Dream can be identified. These include: personal freedom, self-reliance, self-actualization, self-invention, equality, autonomy, success, the living out of religious ideals, economic opportunity, the acquisition of property including home ownership, the Good Life, the draw of the Golden West, new beginnings, personal transformation, economic or social advancement, hope, independence, agency, possibility. Among these ideals and goals certain of them may be seen as compatible, others overlap, while still others may clash and be seen as contradictory. A broad, general and therefore useful definition of the American Dream has been offered by Robert C. Hauhart in his sociological inquiry into the topic: "The American Dream means for many, and perhaps for most, 'doing well' according to one's own standards – materially, spiritually, or in virtually any sense of the words." [7] The final word on the subject will be given to James Truslow Adams, an historian who is credited with the invention of the phrase American Dream. In his one-volume history of the United States, titled *The Epic of America,* Adams provided an explanation of the term as spacious as the country itself, seeing it as referring to the perennial American aspiration to achieve "a better, richer and happier life for all our citizens of every rank." [8]

In approaching the theme of America as it is expressed in Kerouac's writing, I will consider both the author's fiction and autobiographical essays, as well as his letters and personal journal entries. It will, I think, be clear that from the outset the author's treatment of the theme is imbued with a degree of ambivalence and contradiction and that these intensify as the turmoil of American realities alternately confirms and calls into question his idealistic conceptions of his country and his countrymen. As the theme unfolds through Kerouac's various writings, diverse aspects of the American Dream (as listed above) will be seen to be embraced and achieved, only later to be questioned and abandoned, and in their turn replaced by other, deeper dreams.

It was, Kerouac was later to write, during his attendance at Columbia University in the fall of 1940, after having broken his leg during football practice, that he came upon and eagerly read the novels of Thomas Wolfe with their lyrical descriptions of the landscapes of the United States. Wolfe, he wrote, "woke me up to America as a Poem." [9] Early attempts by Kerouac at a literary expression of his all-embracing affection for his country include an experimental prose piece titled "I Have to Pull up my Stakes and Roll, Man," and a free verse poem titled "America in the Night," both written in 1941 and only published posthumously in 1999 in *Atop an Underwood,* a collection of the author's juvenilia. [10] The former piece is a kind of stream-of-consciousness paen to the United States, a long poetic enumeration of things the writer (identifying himself as "Kerouac") loves. These include American clothes, jazz, jitterbugs, newspapers and magazines, sports heroes, race horses, films and film stars, authors and towns and cities all over America. The writer asserts that he feels himself to be "part of the American temper, the American temperament, the American tempo." (113) The poem, "America in the Night," celebrates in Whitmanesque fashion the mystery of the American night with its sleepers, its train whistles, its blues music, its forests and cities.

Drawing upon and deepening the inspiration he received from the novels of Thomas Wolfe, Kerouac began to conceive a private and idiosyncratic devotion to the American landscape and its people, a nascent personal faith according to the terms of which, as he expressed in a letter to a friend written in early 1943, "the essential and everlasting America" abided still – even while the war was in progress and what Kerouac viewed as a shallow disproportionate patriotism ran high – and would endure despite wartime mobilizations, migrations, dislocations and passing distractions. [11] A more expansive statement of his faith in "American destiny" is to be found in an (unpublished) essay he wrote in the fall of 1946. [12] Titled "America in World History," the essay paints in an unfavourable light what the author considers to be a weary and debilitated European culture and civilization in contrast to that of the still youthful and eager United States. Kerouac celebrates American authors (Emerson, Thoreau, Whitman, Wolfe) American music (country music and jazz) and the American character which he sees as spirited and individualistic. He declares that America is to be his theme as an author and that on this matter: "I see no end to my subject and my task." (9) And yet already during that same fall of 1946, the author's vision of America begins to seem somewhat at variance with itself, as he writes in a unpublished piece titled "A Couple of Facts Concerning Laws of Decadence" that intellectual, urban Americans are deracinated and disconnected from natural temporal rhythms and from essential human sympathy. In brief, in this regard, American city-dwellers would seem to have more in common with effete, enervated Europeans than to resemble earnest and vigorous "essential" Americans. [13] Not all Americans, then, nor all places, are in Kerouac's estimation, necessarily to be considered as part of "the essential and everlasting America."

As yet inchoate but coalescing in the imagination of the author at this early stage is a cluster of cultural values and anxieties, including anti-urban currents and a re-assertion of Romantic ideals concerning rootedness and rural life. Kerouac's distaste for the city as a place where essential human values are being undermined and overturned can be seen to resonate with earlier, similar American critiques of city life by – among others – Thomas Jefferson and Henry David Thoreau; while the author's place-attachment and his idealization of common people will be seen to have their roots in English pastoral traditions and Romanticism, in the poetry of William Cowper and William Wordsworth, for example, and in Wordworth's celebrated "Preface to Lyrical Ballads." [14]

Kerouac's travels, his readings in history and his reflections during the years 1948 to 1949 provided further substance to the vision of America taking shape in his mind. In his journals for these years, the author disparages American Anglophiles and Europhiles for their ignorance of and scorn for "the true American culture as found on farms and in small towns and certain smaller cities." [15] In the pages of the same personal journals, he extols what he sees as the reckless, adventurous, expansive spirit of America as embodied in mountain men, pioneers, outlaws, rebels, authors and sportsmen, including Jim Bridger, Jesse James, William F. Cody, Bill Hickock, Sitting Bull, Yellowstone Red, Babe Ruth, Mark Twain and Zane Gray. On a journey by bus through the western states, Kerouac discovers, among Indians, cowhands, miners, gamblers and oldtimers, what he deems to be a "rugged necessary soulfulness." (309) He particularly admires the joyous, generous qualities he perceives in the unpaid crews of young men who clear snow drifts from the highway in the depths of Montana winter, contrasting their high-spirited western helpfulness with the ethos of the east: "Where in the effete-thinking East would men work for others, for nothing, at midnight in howling freezing gales?" (310)

Noteworthy in Kerouac's east versus west and European versus American dichotomies is the degree to which they can be seen to correspond to deep-seated historic patterns in American culture and letters. The western hero – figures such as Leather-stocking, Daniel Boone, Kit Carson and Deadwood Dick – enjoys a favoured place in the American imagination. Such figures are often depicted as "fugitives from civilization," virile and virtuous, intuitive and independent, in contrast to the bankers, merchants and hapless wage laborers, the class-ridden, commerce-and-industry-dominated inhabitants of eastern urban society. [16] Another kind of hero in American tradition – though far less often celebrated in literature and film – is the frontier farmer, "the hero of a myth, of *the* myth of mid-nineteenth century America." (135) In common with the myth of the western hero, this agrarian embodiment of an American heroic ideal—an independent, industrious, honest common man operating a family farm – affirms that "the destiny of this country leads her away from Europe toward the agricultural interior of the continent," (260) and away from the poverty, inequality and materialistic excesses of the urban industrial Atlantic seaboard.

A literary parallel to the opposition in American thought between urbanist and anti-urbanist attitudes, and between East and West, can be seen in the tension between American literary schools as identified and described by the late critic Philip Rahv in a landmark essay titled "Paleface and Redskin." [17] Rahv argued that "historically, American writers appear to group themselves around two polar types," which he named as Palefaces and Redskins: the former refined, intellectual, patrician and inclining to a European-style sensibility, the latter "primarily emotional, spontaneous," and revelling in a vigorous, plebian Americanness; the former group represented by Henry James, the latter by Walt Whitman. (252) Perhaps this psychic division may not be as sharply defined as Rahv – for schematic, polemical purposes – argued, but it is clear that in terms of the attitudes and attributes that are said to characterize the two warring camps, Kerouac clearly inclines to the Redskin clan, celebrating energy and experience over form and reflection, preferring the saloon to the salon.

Two inter-related major themes pervade Kerouac's first published novel, *The Town and the City*: the rural versus urban conflict and the theme of America. [18] The conflict between the values, customs and conventions of a small, rural community and those of a large urban center, prefigured in the novel's title, is established in the opening pages of the book, where an anonymous third-person narrator describes in idyllic images the town of Galloway, located among woods, hills and a river in the northeastern United States. Galloway, we are told by the narrator, is "a town rooted in earth and the ancient pulse of life and work and death, that makes its people townspeople and not city people." (5) The narrator's description of Galloway and environs is characterized by a cluster of attractive and appealing modifying words, such as "fresh," "soft," "quiet," "sedate," "smooth," "placid," and "calm." (pp. 5-6) In these bucolic surroundings, the members of the Martin family, the central narrative focus of the novel, are depicted as thriving.

Young Peter Martin is the first figure in the novel to understand the life-giving, spirit-nourishing significance of geographical rootedness and cultural embeddedness. Having attended a distant preparatory school and then a university, then returning by train to Galloway after long absence to spend a Christmas with his family, he experiences an epiphany of deep affinity and attachment to the landscape and the town of his birth and his childhood: "... he was rediscovering his earth, which he had been away from too long, it seemed. ... He wanted it back for himself again and for always. It was his land, his own land." (146) Weighing this forceful and profound new awareness of attraction and identity against the subjects he has been studying at the university, he realizes that the latter are no more than shallow and inconsequential forms of information in comparison to "the plain powerful knowledge" he suddenly possesses: "Nothing that the university taught him could match for him the power and wisdom of his own kind of people, who lived and drew their breath in this rugged land joyous with tidings of towns, plain, homely, genuine and familiar." (147)

By the disruptions of war and by marriage, the various Martin children are eventually scattered to every corner and coast of the country, while the remaining core of the family – the Martin parents and their youngest son – is forced by economic circumstances to move to New York city. An ominous portent of their final fate in the city is the large advertisement painted long ago on a windowless wall that dominates the view from their basement apartment, a commercial mural depicting an "indistinct, faded, huge man holding his head in despair." (344) Following a brief, initial optimism about his new situation in the city, George Martin soon senses his acute isolation far from home and among strangers. He is, he realizes, "more alone at this time of his life than he had ever been ... an irreparably lonely man." (351)

The extremes of poverty and wealth to which George Martin is witness in the streets of New York city, the seeming impassivity and indifference of the city's inhabitants, the rush and rudeness of the thronging subways and sidewalks, all stand in stark contrast to his tender memories of the small towns of his youth and manhood. Consonant with George Martin's despondent mood, the narrator's descriptions of the city form a semantic field dominated by negative modifying words – "mournful," "faded," "dirtied," "sooty," "dark," "somber," "hollow," "sickly," "terrifying," "cracked" "bleak" – and by imagery of waste and ruin: "beaten dust" and "debris," "rubbish fires" and a "junkyard," "busted windows" and "dusty windows," "filthy clothes" and "rheumy eyes." Privy to the inmost thoughts and emotions of George Martin, the narrator tells us that "the dark and serious sorrows of New York at night froze his heart." (352) Severed from his origins, his native soil and the roots of his being, George Martin sickens and dies in the city.

In a similar manner, young Peter Martin, guileless and good-natured product of Galloway, now a merchant seaman caught up in the war, experiences among his new urbane acquaintances in New York City cynicism, decadence, crime and murder. In consequence of his exposure to such sordidness and moral squalor, he comes to feel only an "empty bitter horror," (406) and realizes that, like that of his father, his own life "had come to a dead end in the city." (462)

A final contrast between the values of the town and those of the city occurs in the novel's closing chapters when the surviving members of the Martin family are temporarily reunited upon earth of home to attend their father's funeral and burial – his longed-for return to his native soil. The country relatives and local family friends who gather for the ceremony are described as a "strong, determined" (497) kindly clan, well acquainted with and accepting of life's uncertainties and its everlasting certainties. Restless Joe Martin, the oldest of the Martin children, returned from the war, resolves to settle in the area, farm the land and raise a family – a strong, concluding affirmation in the novel of the deep, human meanings of the town and the country over the confusions, excesses and atomization attendant upon modern urban life.

A powerful yearning suffuses Kerouac's debut novel – the allure of America, the pull of its distances, the mystery of its vast and varied landscapes, and the compelling fascination of something inexpressible, something indefinable, something subtle but vital, something at once abiding and elusive in the American experience. Joe, the eldest brother of the Martin brood, feels this fascination but can neither grasp nor express what it is: "It had no name, he did not know what it was." (68) Interspersed throughout the plot action and dialogue of *The Town and the City* are lyrical descriptive passages, celebrating "the wild carelessness of a savage rhapsodic America in its shouting youthfulness." (54) Again, it is principally Joe among the Martins, who senses and responds to the magnetic attraction of America, even as a boy longing "to see sublime mountains, massive canyons, great mountain forests ... lakes ... deserts and mesas and the great rivers." (67) As soon as he is old enough and able to do so, Joe takes a job as a long-distance truck driver, savouring the roadside diners, the gas stations, the long highways, the nights and dawns on the road, exulting in the power and speed of his vehicle, rejoicing in the freedom and the beauty of the American road, riding: "windows open to the soft Spring night with all its odors of loamy fields and flowers and the sharp pungent smell of exhaust fumes on the highway, and the heat of the highway itself cooling under the stars, and the fried-food smells floating in the air from all the places." (92) Drawn by the irresistible pull of the continent, the seductive sense of sheer physical space, Joe highjacks the truck he's driving in order to travel west, to travel further, to lay eyes on ever more of the land ahead of him on the highway. Then, fired from his job, and driven by a nameless, restless urgency to move and to see, he leaves Galloway to hitch-hike from coast to coast and border to border across the country.

Not merely in the wonder of distance and the magic of movement is the mythic significance of America conveyed by

Kerouac in the novel. The author finds poetry in race tracks and football stadiums, in family meals and foggy April rain, in music from a radio and in the tender charm of a small town summer night: "all cricket-stirring and soft, under tall drooping trees and the sultry stars of night in June." (215) In all these things, the author implies, there is a felt meaning, a depth, a poignance, a feeling both of longing and belonging, an aching sense of yearning and of loss. *The Town and the City* is, thus, at once a celebration of and an elegy for what was lost in America during the war years – including rootedness and community – and an urgent summons to fare forward toward an undiscovered America. This division can be seen in the novel's ambiguous resolution where Joe Martin grounds himself on earth of home with the aim of raising a family, even while Peter Martin embarks on a solitary restless quest westward across the American continent.

In contrast to the lyrical affirmations of *The Town and the City*, a grimmer, more somber spirit threads through *Visions of Cody*. [19] With shifting moods and tones, this innovative novel – written about three years after Kerouac finished revisions on *The Town and the City* – follows the narrator's observations of American life in cities on both coasts of the United States and at points along the continent between them. The opening scenes of the book take place in New York city which – as in *The Town and the City* – is depicted in terms of seamy squalor and psychic sterility. Longing to travel west, but marooned in New York city, the disconsolate narrator Jack Duluoz wanders the streets, among buildings that are " broken ... spotty ... dusty ... scarred ... chipped ... weatherbeaten ... ragged ... filthy," and upon sidewalks littered with old newspapers, cigarette butts and banana peels, and bespattered with "puke" and "piss." And, like the inhabitants of London in Blake's poem *London* or those in T.S. Eliot's *The Waste Land,* the faces Duluoz beholds in the city of New York are "closed and grave" (27) "grim and sullen." (29) Likewise, the lives that he observes in subways and streets, diners, shops and offices seem to him pinched and petty, preoccupied with trivial things, numbed by pointless distractions.

Yet hitchhiking and travelling by bus westward to Denver and San Francisco, Duluoz discovers on his journey little that can be construed as heartening. Everywhere are lonely soldiers and sailors, blinkered businessmen, lost souls, hopeless winos, broken black men, B-girls, tubercular okies, Mexican hoodlums, anxious immigrants and worried waitresses. Even the landscape of the west seems to him defiled and depleted: "sooty girders and worn old black planks of railroad bridges behind warehouses ... cinder yards ... nameless tunnels, alleys ... ash heaps, miniature dumps ... filthy covered-with-rags plazas ... bleak black branches." (103) Nothing to be found here that might announce the imminence of that longed-for America whose "alabaster cities gleam undimmed by human tears." [20]

Two key passages in the novel treat the status of American dreams: the neon versus redbrick section (pp. 104-113) and the Joan Rawshanks chapter (pp. 318-336.) Ann Charters was the first to direct readers' attention to the centrality and metaphoric import of the neon versus redbrick imagery in *Visions of Cody.* [21] With acute insight, Charters interprets the opposition between the two images here as suggesting the fate of ideals and dreams of life in collision with implacable realities. In this harsh world of hard material facts dreams are inevitably broken, hopes are unavoidably shattered. Like an *ignis fatuus* or fool's fire, the bright neons beckon to us, enticing us, inciting and promising fulfilment of our desires, but ever and always hidden behind the seductive colored glow of the neon is the blank, unyielding brick wall, marking the dead-end of dreams.

The Joan Rawshanks section treats of an occurrence in the foggy night streets of San Francisco when a movie sequence is being filmed on location. A film crew, technicians, various assistants and a director are assembled to record a sequence starring a once-famous-now-fading film star, Joan Rawshanks. Crowded on sidewalks nearby stand scores of entranced on-lookers. The episode records and reflects upon the way in which the spectators – each a unique mind and life, each endowed with a capacity for transformation and redemption – allow themselves to be reduced to passive fascination and vicarious gratification. The illusory, insubstantial nature of the display on which the spectators stare with such reverent interest is suggested by the ever-changing names of the film star (Joan Ashplant, Joan Clawthighs, Joan Crawfish) in the course of the narrative and by the presence on the set of a man who resembles Leon Edel, a deceased film star, and who therefore receives the deference and esteem once accorded his celebrated late lookalike. And yet the unnamed double of Leon Edel is but a facsimile, mere surface appearance devoid of true self-identity, a species of impostor. In a similar manner, Joan Rawshanks, under a heavy layer of makeup and moving and assuming facial expressions according to the precise instructions of the director, portrays a person she is not and emotions she does not feel. The film itself, of course, is (or ultimately will be) an elaborate fabrication, an imitation of life, and for future film audiences a substitution for life. Duluoz, witness to these events, perceives both the wistful life-famished desires of the onlookers (comparing them on page 329 to the jaded, gaping throng of onlookers in Nathaniel West's novel, *The Day of the Locust*) as well as the isolation and private griefs of the aging film star and the "great hollow sorrow and strange emptiness and ... lostness" (321) of the affable-seeming, elegant double of the deceased actor. Significantly, both participants and onlookers alike are veiled in fog, enveloped in a gray, opaque obscurity, suggesting vague, purblind lives without clear vision, lives faint and indistinct.

A more explicit criticism of American life in the novel occurs when Duluoz contemplates the unhappy childhood of his friend, Cody Pomeray, an impoverished orphan at one time wanted by the Denver police for his petty thefts, alone and hiding in Pueblo. The vision of his unfortunate friend's early sorrows causes Duluoz to ponder the woes of fugitives, outcasts and unfortunates across the vast continent. "America, the word, the sound is the sound of my unhappiness," he declares in bitterness, "the pronunciation of my beat and stupid grief – my happiness has no such name as America." (118) He then unrolls a catalog of tragic fates and brutal features in the life of the American nation: the earnest but despised immigrant, the vicious plainclothesman, the staggering drunk in his defeat, "murderous dogs snarling behind wire fences" to protect private property, the cruising police car, the myriad forlorn and lonely souls in a land where "nobody cares," the lowly restaurant dishwasher, the miserable "corner newsstand midget," the tragedy of the poor and of Negroes, of nightshift workers and beggars.

Yet notwithstanding the lamentations and complaints, the disappointment and displeasure concerning aspects of America as expressed by the author in various passages and sections of *Visions of Cody,* the novel also celebrates the beauty and the vibrant life and "immense indefinable charm of the wideopen free sprawling America." (21) Indeed, at one point, the narrator is moved to assert: "I dig a 1000 things in America." (61) Among the thousand things Duluoz digs are the many shapes and features of the United States, the plateaux and the great mountains, the lakes and rivers, the remote country towns "laid out neat and bright," (422) the cacti and adobe walls, the pines and cliffs and canyons. He also celebrates the saloons and highways, the dim poolhalls of Denver and rickety wooden piers of Los Angeles, the plangent sound of "guitars tinkling softly across hillbilly hollows" (427) and plaintive songs heard over a car radio, kindly bus drivers and companionable servicemen and barelegged house-wives hanging wash on backyard clothes lines. "I loved the blue dawns over racetracks," he hymns, "and made a bet Ioway was sweet like its name, my heart went out to lonely sounds in the misty springtime night of wild sweet America in her powers, the wetness on the wire fence bugled me to belief, I stood on sandpiles with an open soul." (462) In the tradition of Walt Whitman and Thomas Wolfe, Kerouac pronounces a poetic paean to America.

Duluoz also extols those he sees as modern American heroes, contemporary exemplary expressions of the American spirit. Two such figures are Cody Pomeray and Lester Young. In Cody (whose forename, of course, connects him with William F. Cody and the American frontier) Duluoz recognizes an alternative embodiment of that American archetype, the self-made man. [22] Cody comes from the very bottom of the social ladder, the motherless son of a drunken itinerant barber, growing up in Denver flophouses, repeatedly sentenced to reform school and later to jail. Yet he is driven to better himself, casting himself over the philosophy of Arthur Schopenhauer and the study of metaphysics, reading Marcel Proust, even while becoming an accomplished athlete (and car thief.) Although ragged Cody does not rise to riches, he does attain relative economic security working as a railroad brakeman, purchasing a house in which to live with his wife and children, and preserving at the same time a species of bohemian integrity with his marijuana and his literary, musical and metaphysical interests. Duluoz acknowledges Cody's many flaws, but honors him for his pilgrim soul, his nobility of spirit.

As an African-American, Lester Young's origins are even more impoverished and more marginal, more utterly unpromising than those of Cody, but he, too, is a self-made man: rising by talent and willpower from poverty and obscurity to become a musical innovator who is, in Duluoz' view, the originator of modern jazz. Lester Young represents, for Duluoz, "the greatness of America in a single Negro musician." (456) He is likened by Duluoz to an American river flowing from its humble headwaters to become a powerful waterway, a mighty current coursing through the heart of the American nation, bearing "muddy news from the land and a roar of subterranean excitement that is like the vibration of the entire land." (456)

Through the medium of radio, the potent, passionate, inspired music of Lester Young reaches the distant ears of young Cody Pomeray, suffusing his soul and shaping his character. In this manner, Duluoz' chosen exemplars of a new American heroism are linked, the outcast dark hero secretly fostering the orphaned white boy. A further connection between Cody and Lester Young is made in the novel by the ardent effusions of Lionel, an English jazz fan, who sees in Cody with his excited postures and gestures, his wild laughter and manic talk, the kinetic, verbal equivalent of a jazz musician soloing, pouring forth without restraint his naked soul to the world. "America's real mad," Lionel pronounces approvingly, "Lester ... and guys like Cody in America. Crazy." (460) (Note: in hip parlance "mad" and "crazy" were terms of high approbation.) Both Lester Young and Cody Pomeray are thus seen to personify a peculiarly American spirit, something radical, exhilarating, unbridled, vital and original, "a joyous revolt from convention, custom, authority, boredom, even sorrow – from everything that would confine the soul of man and hinder its riding free on the air."[23] Amid the bystanders and onlookers of the nation, arise two modern prophets giving a new direction and a new dimension to an old American dream.

Already, then, in *Visions of Cody*, we begin to discern the lineaments of those kinds of Americans of whom the author disapproves and those of whom he approves. In the former category are the spectators, the distracted and complacent, the torporous and resigned, those living manicured lives, those pursuing power, status or material wealth, those who are oblivious to what is vital in life, those accepting of the conventions and limits in which they live, those whose lives are bereft of depth and real meaning. That same "mass of men," in short, who according to Thoreau, "live lives of quiet desperation."[24] The kind of Americans favoured by Kerouac are those awake to the world, those of independent mind and untamed spirit, those capable of awe and actively pursuing awe, those seeking meaning, those exceeding and expanding the boundaries of ordinary perception and consciousness. (There is something here reminiscent of the traditional opposition in American culture and literature between frontiersmen and settlers.) These clashing categories of Americans – with all that they imply of beliefs and behaviours – continue to appear throughout Kerouac's work.

Book of Sketches is a collection of notations, observations, reflections, resolutions, ideas for books and films, memories, vignettes, lists, inventories and enumerations, descriptions, dreams and poems assembled from Kerouac's notebooks from the summer of 1952 to December 1954. [25] The text was prepared by the author for publication in 1959, but remained unpublished until 2006. Here in fragmentary form are straightforward declarations and general outlines of certain themes treated in the author's earlier writings and to be treated in subsequent writings. Indeed, in the *Book of Sketches* can be seen something of a credo of Kerouac's preoccupations at this stage of his vocation as a writer. The fundamental concept with which Kerouac works is one derived from his reading of Oswald Spengler's *The Decline of the West*, but adapted and recast according to his own interpretation of human life and human history. [26]

Kerouac uses the term *fellaheen* (Arabic meaning ploughman or tiller of the soil) to denote a universal indigenous peasantry, exploited, despised, economically and socially submerged, yet constituting the basis of human life, the foundation on which all else rests. He views the fellaheen as the genuine, original, primary and final cohort of humanity. They are seen by him as existing below history, that is below civilized life with its technology, luxury, commerce, industry, institutions, cities, nation states, empires, and wars. They may be conscripted, victimized, constrained and coerced by the forces of history and civilization but they remain forever apart from those forces, enduring in tenacious irrelevance. The fellaheen pursue agriculture and live in harmony with the natural world. They wish only to be left unmolested in their modest human pursuits. One day, Kerouac foresees, because of the pervasive corruption and decadence of civilized urban life and the aggression of nation states, the world of history will inevitably collapse and fall into ruin. Then, as prophesied by Jesus Christ in the Sermon on the Mount: "The meek shall inherit the earth." (Matthew 5:5) The fellaheen, the humble, rightful owners of the world, will then again resume possession of it.

To Kerouac (as for Spengler) the West is "Faustian," that is to say that – like Goethe's or Marlowe's Faust – it has exchanged its soul for material benefits, for knowledge and power. And the United States of America, in his view, is – in its refinements, its superfluities, its dependence upon technology – pre-eminent among Western nations. Throughout *Book of Sketches* are laments for the "lost spiritualities of America" for a country "empty of meaning but rich, fruitful, golden." (172) In scattered entries, Kerouac deplores the seductions of advertising and consumerism, the tyrany of standardized time and work-regimented lives, the soul-deadening distractions of commercial radio and television, and the reduction of the populace to willing serfs of The Machine: "Machine Humanbeings" (184) "Americans who only think in terms of paranoia and oil," (101) accomplices in the Faustian bargain, abettors of their own undoing. He extols, instead, the virtues of the dispossessed American Indians, such as the Pomo tribe of California, who "spoke to spiders and hawks and thanked the ground they slept on." (245) At one point, the author angrily declares "Gad I hate America with a passionate intensity," (148) though when assembling *Book of Sketches* some years after this sentiment was originally recorded in his notebook, Kerouac adds a parenthetical apology: "Written when I was a railroad brakeman covered with soot mad as hell in 1952: I apologize now, America, in 1959, for such filthy bitterness but that's what I said then, and meant it." (149)

The "essential and everlasting America" to which the author paid respect in the 1943 letter to a friend as quoted above, still abides; it is still to be found. "The Life Flow," Kerouac writes, yet proceeds "underneath this junk." (279) The countryside (proximate to The Life Flow) is again contrasted to the city: "the City fattens on the blood of Towns" (179) and "The Agrarian American is the strongest American because nearest to Fellaheen condition." (192) An image that encapsulates the disastrous, destructive separation of the city from The Life Flow is a description of half-a-dozen "pathetic little pots" on the window of a New York city tenement apartment. (310) The roots and stems of the potted plants are dead, the leaves dry and dead, the plants "completely bent and despairing," depleted to "clutters of wrinkled huskleaf "(310-311) Perhaps it is a measure of the author's disenchantment at this time with urban life and with America that he seems seriously to consider pursuing a life as a goatherd. (280) He also expresses his admiration for the winos and hobos he encounters who have abandoned ambitions and materialistic desires for a life of independence. In consonance with Kerouac's expectations of the inevitable decline of American civilization, his descriptions in the notebooks depict weeds, broken glass, cast off shoes, junkyards, forlorn shacks, unsavoury graffiti, old rusty plows and cars, nameless metal debris, "all spectral iron hell," (182) objects dismal and tragic, sad artefacts of sad lives, portents of an impending "apocalypse of the fellaheen," and "The Millennium of the Meek." (176)

While "the apocalypse of the fellaheen" is an essential core theme in *On the Road* – a deep-rooted conviction underlying the narrative – it is first explicitly articulated in the climactic chapters of the novel dealing with the journey into Mexico. [27] In the main, *On the Road* treats what might be termed the outward appendages or extensions of the fellaheen theme, the ways in which this conflict of values and attitudes manifests itself in aspects of American social life at mid-century. Already in the opening chapter of the novel, opposing ways of understanding life in the world are assigned to representative figures. The group with which the narrator, Sal Paradise, is initially affiliated (but with which he has grown disenchanted) consists of urban intellectuals subscribing to various ideologies (Nietzsche, surrealism, psychoanalysis) all with the common denominator of a complacent, all-pervading negativity. Sal has fallen under the influence of their pessimism, absorbing their despondency as if by osmosis, coming to feel that his life is "stultified" (7) and that "everything is dead." (1) The catalytic stranger to whom Sal is drawn as representing a potential redeemer from the unhappy psychic condition that afflicts him is Dean Moriarty who is in every way the antithesis of a sophisticated, cynical, educated, east coast, urban intellectual. He is a westerner, a lumpen prole, a car thief, a jailbird, a ranch hand, a young man of high energy and keen appetites, hungry for sex, for ideas, for friends and adventures. Dean is imbued with a life-affirming vitality and a zestful optimism, the very things that Sal requires to rescue him from the dejection that has descended upon him like a net. Thus early, the terms of the novel are set: sensuality versus abstraction, body versus intellect, mobility versus stasis, nature versus civilization, the kind of Americans Kerouac esteems and those he does not.

In this latter category – in addition to jaundiced urban intellectuals – can also be included those who are seen by Sal as pursuing prosaic, circumscribed lives, lives without passion or curiosity, who in the face of the awesome mystery of existence can only "yawn" and say "commonplace things," (5) seemingly oblivious or indifferent to the deeper meaning and higher beauty of life. Examples in the novel of such impercipient inertia and misplaced attention, include the gawking celebrity-beguiled tourists haunting the streets of Hollywood, standing on sidewalks "gaping for sight of some movie star," (80) and the irredeemable "squares," ever-guarded, ever-fretful, ever pre-occupied with incidental inessentials as life passes them by, of whom Dean observes: "they need to worry and betray time with urgencies false and otherwise, purely anxious and whiny, their souls really won't be at peace unless they can latch on to an established and proven worry." (197) A further example of life-denying propriety is that of the conventional young woman encountered in a bus by Sal, so irredeemably dull and un-imaginative as to provoke near despair in his soul: "Her great dark eyes surveyed me with emptiness and a kind of chagrin that reached back generations and generations in her blood from not having done what was crying to be done." (232) She seems baffled by Sal's questions, as he attempts to hint at deeper unsatisfied yearnings and ultimate meanings. Significantly, she concludes their conversation with a yawn.

If the excessively intellectual and the inveterately dull are to be pitied for their incapacity to apprehend the environing Mystery, there is in *On the Road* another class of persons who are to be steered clear of as far as possible: those who enforce the law. Policemen and security guards are experienced by Sal and Dean as meddlesome and authoritarian, caught up in a hyper-masculine code and an impelling need to exercise power over others. Near Washington D.C. and again in Pennsylvania, the two companions are stopped by traffic policemen and given heavy fines for speeding – "in spite of the fact that we were going about thirty." (112) In Benson, Arizona, a suspicious police officer pulls a gun on Dean. Following these incidents, Sal is moved to remark that "The American police are involved in psychological warfare against those Americans who don't frighten them with imposing papers and threats ... it peers out of musty windows and wants to inquire about everything, and can make crimes if the crimes don't exist to its satisfaction." (127) Epitomizing in the novel the type of person drawn to such work are the ex-Alcatraz guard and Sledge, the aspiring Texas Ranger, with whom Sal works for a time as a security guard. The former is "retired but unable to keep away from the atmospheres that had nourished his dry soul all his life," (60) and is much given to fond reminiscences of his twenty-two years as a prison guard and of more recent injuries he has inflicted upon arrestees. The latter, Sledge, has rigged himself out "like a Texas Ranger of old. He wore a revolver down low, with ammunition belt, and carried a small quirt of some kind, and pieces of leather hanging everywhere, like a walking torture chamber ... He desperately wanted to make arrests." (61) In the time-honoured American "pursuit of happiness" on which Sal and Dean are embarked in *On the Road,* officious law enforcement officers are seen to be a recurrent hindrance, repeatedly infringing upon and impeding the quest for the Dream.

In *On the Road,* American cities are once again portrayed by Kerouac as sites of all that is pitiless, hopeless and destructive in American life. Los Angeles is characterized as "the loneliest and most brutal of American cities ... LA is a jungle." (79) New York is a locus of "absolute madness ... with its millions and millions hustling forever for a buck among themselves, the mad dream – grabbing, taking, giving, sighing, dying, just so they could be buried in those awful cemetery sites beyond Long Island City." (98) San Francisco is perceived as being inhabited by a rum bunch of bunglers, duds and has-beens: "Everybody looked like a broken-down movie extra, withered starlet, disenchanted stunt-men, midget auto-racers, poignant California characters with their end-of-the-continent sadness, handsome, decadent, Casanova-ish men, puffy eyed motel blondes, hustlers, pimps, whores, masseurs, bellhops – a lemon lot." (158) Even Dean's hometown, the city of Denver is compared to the Biblical city of Sodom: "And Denver receded back of us like the city of salt, her smokes breaking up in the air and dissolving to our sight." (255) As this last image suggests, the environmental pollution and spiritual pollution of the cities would seem to be mutually reflexive.

Beyond the dense, dirty cities, beyond the congestion and the competition, the winners and losers of urban life, are mountains and clouds, rivers and plains, deserts and forests, and a myriad of American lives scattered across the vastness of the continent. There is magnificence, majesty and mystery. There are the stars above Wyoming, mist on the Blue Ridge mountains, and there is Strawberry Pass and "the mighty wall of Berthoud Pass," (200) the Mississippi "the great brown father of waters," and the Kanawha River, the Monongahela, the Shenandoah and the Susquehanna; there are the many towns Tehachapi, Ogallala, Three Forks, Longmont, Ashland, Salome, and the fields and farmhouses of Indiana and Iowa, and there are long-haul truck drivers, ranchers and fellaheen farm laborers. And, although – metaphorically and perhaps also literally speaking – the nation is occasionally somewhat "ragged" and sometimes "tumbledown," America in Sal's road-wise eyes is still the "promised land," (76) it is still "holy America." (140) Sal refers to his homeland affectionately as "my American continent" (72) and at one point exults that ahead of him and Dean as they travel west lies "the whole country like an oyster for us to open and the pearl was there, the pearl was there." (129) America for Kerouac is still "the endless poem." (242)

In his urgent travels to and fro across the United States, Sal invokes as guides "the pioneers" (9) and heroic American figures such as Ben Franklin, George Washington, William Bradford and Daniel Boone. (97) Among contemporary Americans, Sal most admires individualists and free-spirits, the humble and good-hearted, the boisterous, lively and animated, figures such as the "rawhide oldtimer Nebraska farmer" whom he encounters in a roadside diner, whose laughter and genial disposition seem to Sal to embody "the spirit of the West." (17) Another such figure is Mr. Snow, an African-American man whose laugh is "positively and finally the one greatest laugh in the all this world… a whooping triumphant call." (56 -7) There are also the two shy, "smiling, cheerful" (20) young blond farm boys from Minnesota driving a flatbed truck and picking up every hitchhiker along the highway, and the kindly interracial couple in Los Angeles who generously host Sal and his girlfriend, Terry. And, of course, Sal prizes in his friend Dean what he sees as inspiring qualities of openness and energy, optimism and enthusiasm, rebelliousness and an adventurous spirit, and – in spite of multitudinous sins – a curious elemental and essential innocence.

Sal sees in Dean a kind of semi-fellaheen or white fellaheen, a displaced, dispossessed Irish peasant, disdained and outcast in mechanized America, a primitive or natural man, spontaneous, antifaustian in a Faustian social order. Dean pursues his simple, sensual life at the margins of American culture, indifferent to laws, customs and conventions, evading claims made upon him by society, government, institutions and history, his spoken aim: "a whole life of non-interference with the wishes of others, including politicians and the rich." (239) In contrast to the myriad grimly striving, aspiring inhabitants of the cities and the effete urban intellectuals with their "tired bookish or political or psychoanalytical" mental structures, Dean, we are told, is concerned only with the essentials of life, he: "just raced in society, eager for bread and love; he didn't care one way or the other." (7) In terms of values, attitudes and behaviours ("He drove like an Indian" p. 286) Dean is allied in Sal's mind with other ethnic and racial groups in *On the Road*, groups treated as insignificant and peripheral in American society but admired by Sal for what he sees as their unaffected, languid, reverent style of life: the Mexican-American agricultural labourers of the San Joaquin Valley, the African-Americans, Mexicans and Japanese workers of Denver. And, of course, the innocent, impoverished Indians of Mexico. Such people, Sal believes, intrinsically recognize what is truly of consequence in life and what is inessential and insubstantial.

The musical accompaniment of the quest for transcendence running through *On the Road* is jazz – frantic, subtle, heart-stirring, spirit-lifting, earthy and ethereal, visceral and soulful, urgent, passionate, cathartic, sacramental, enrapturing, joyous jazz. In the exultations and affirmations of jazz, Sal and Dean find intimations of unnameable sacred energies, which they can only speak of as "IT." Jazz performances are for them like shamanic séances impelling them toward a final – if ever elusive – gnosis. In jazz they discover the sovereign power of music "to break through into a non-physical mode of being, and there to develop in a life of unexpected fullness." [28] This potent, numinous music, rooted in the isolation and alienation of the African-American experience, becomes for Sal and Dean – for Kerouac – a universal expression of our common human bereftness, our common exile on this dark earth of sorrows.

Spiritual yearnings and intuitions in *On the Road* are also expressed in terms of Eastern religio-philosophical traditions.

This can be seen in the remarkable revelation experienced by Sal in San Francisco when penniless, homeless and hungry, he is seized by a vision in which he steps out of "chronological time into timeless shadows ... the holy void of uncreated emptiness," there to confront the radiance of "Mind Essence," and recall his numberless births and deaths on earth. (162) Later in the novel, he makes an allusion to "the Prince of Dharma," (211) and observes of human fate on earth and the prospect of heaven: "what's heaven? what's earth? All in the mind." (233) Both Sal's vision and these later comments would appear to suggest a more than casual acquaintance with and attraction to Buddhist thought. Similarly, Dean's ultimate philosophical perspective – an active passivity and a trusting resignation – is seen by Sal as being "Taoist" in nature. (239) Even wayward Dean, then, would seem in his own fashion to have embraced "the Way." These separate strands of Eastern religious and philosophical thought threading through *On the Road,* are woven into a clear and colorful pattern in *The Dharma Bums.* [29]

Strange to say, Eastern spirituality is something of an American Dream. That is to say that spiritual fulfilment is, of course, foremost among the earliest and most fundamental of American dreams, and that a fascination with Hindu and Buddhist texts, such as *The Bhagavad Gita* and *The Lotus Sutra* dates from the American Transcendentalist movement of the 1840s. Figures seminal for the shape and direction of American thought, including Ralph Waldo Emerson, Henry David Thoreau and Walt Whitman all drew inspiration from Eastern spiritual traditions. Indeed, Whitman's poem "Passage to India," prophesies the destiny of the United States as a bridge between the West and the East, connecting the spiritual insights of the West to those of ancient India, linking the Western philosophical heritage: "to primal thought, to wisdom's birth." [30] This deep-seated affinity of American intellectual and literary currents with Eastern spiritual traditions may serve as a cultural context within which *The Dharma Bums* may be situated.

Curious and incongruous as it may seem, there are also certain parallels and correspondences to be found between those original American dreamers, the Puritans, and the loose coterie of mid-twentieth century west coast American Buddhists as depicted in Kerouac's *The Dharma Bums*. In broad terms, the two spiritually-oriented groups share some essential impulses and goals. The Puritans, it will be remembered, were "separatists," who seceded from the Church of England, undertook "an errand into the wilderness," as Samuel Danforth characterized their mission, and attempted to establish a spiritual community of "saints" that would serve as an ideal model in a corrupt world. [31] A central tenet of their behaviour was to live simply with no vanity, no competition and few possessions. They prescribed plain clothing, plain housing, plain speech. In a similar manner, the Dharma Bums secede or separate themselves from the affluent, consumerist-oriented world of the postwar era and attempt to found an exemplary community, one without competition and vanity, one whose members live modestly in rented shacks or homemade cabins and possess scarcely more than the essentials packed in their rucksacks. Like the Puritans, their mission is spiritual in nature. They hope that their example will serve to attract others to their beliefs and their way of life and will ultimately inspire in American society a revolution of values, "a rucksack revolution." As the Puritans referred to themselves as "saints," the Dharma Bums refer to each other as bhikkus and bodisattvas. And in common with the Puritans, they esteem plain speech: "the true language of this country which is the language of the working men, railroad men, loggers." (74) There are, to be sure, significant differences in the attitudes of the Puritans and those of the Dharma Bums with regard to sexual behaviour, revelry and nature. To the former, the wilderness was the domain of Satan, dangerous, diabolical, while for the Dharma Bums nature is seen as sacred, redemptive, a remnant of Paradise. Yet separated by more than 300 years and the length of a continent, both Puritans and Dharma Bums perceive themselves as bearers of a new truth, agents of anticipatory consciousness, catalysts for the accomplishment of a dream.

The central tension informing *The Dharma Bums* is the opposition of two groups of Americans, two types, two sets of values. The protagonists of the novel are the narrator, Ray Smith, his friend and mentor, Japhy Ryder, and their circle of bohemian-Buddhist companions. The antagonists (or negative examples) of the novel whose attitudes and aspirations are disparaged by the dharma bums, are those among the American populace who are seen to have adopted – at the cost of freedom, curiosity and possibility – the suburban, materialist, consumer-conformist style of life. Early in *The Dharma Bums,* Ray reflects that colleges are little more than "grooming schools for the middle-class non-identity which usually finds its perfect expression on the outskirts of the campus in rows of well-to-do houses with lawns and television sets in each living room with everybody looking at the same thing and thinking the same thing." (39) Similarly, Japhy diagnoses what he perceives as a pervasive malaise of the spirit afflicting his countrymen whom he believes to have yielded "to the general demand that they consume production, and therefore have to work for the privilege of consuming all that crap they didn't really want anyway such as refrigerators, TV sets, cars ... hair oils and deodorants." (97) Walking alone at night along the suburban streets of America, Sal notes with sorrow and some alarm "house after house on both sides of the street each with the lamplight of the living room shining golden, and inside the little blue square of the television, each living family riveting its attention on probably one show; nobody talking; silence in the yards; dogs barking at you because you pass on human feet instead of on wheels," (104) and "cute suburban cottages that couldn't see me because they were all looking at television." (219) Such scenes as these are considered by Ray to be evidence of an insidious passivity and conformity becoming ever more prevalent in American society, ominous portents of a future in which "the Master Switch" (104) will monitor and control all human thought and behaviour.

Hitch-hiking across the American continent, travelling from west to east and back again and from south to north, Ray gives ear to the confidences of the various men who offer him rides, men who acknowledge the absurdity of the hedonic treadmill on which they find themselves caught. There is the long-haul truck driver – a family man, owner of a home, two cars and a two-car garage – who admits to Ray: "Here I am killin myself drivin this rig back and forth from Ohio to L.A. and I make more money than you ever had in your whole life as a hobo, but you're the one who enjoys life. " (129) And there is the salesman who ruefully confides: "Three hundred and sixty days out of the year we get bright sunshine here in El Paso and my wife just bought a clothes dryer!" (157-58) Even Ray's brother-in-law adheres unthinkingly and obstinately to a narrow materialist-money-oriented system of values, defending with indignation to Ray his practice of keeping his unhappy dog chained alone in the backyard day and night: "I've got too much money invested in that dog to untie him from his chain." (143) This image of a hapless dog forever chained solely for pecuniary reasons seems to encapsulate neatly the novel's theme of freedom versus materialism. Significantly, pathetically, the brother-in-law can neither free himself from – nor even perceive – the invisible chain he has forged for himself and by which his spirit is tethered.

In clear contrast to the unflatteringly portrayed lives of the consumer-conformists in all their somnolent, circumscribed sameness is Kerouac's depiction of the dharma bums, principally Ray and Japhy (but also Sean Monahan and Christine.) Their concerns are spiritual in nature. They meditate, pray and seek spiritual knowledge in the reading of sacred texts. They also enjoy active social and sexual lives, much drink and laughter, and undertake exhilarating mountaineering expeditions. They savour simple pleasures (hot dogs and beans cooked over a driftwood fire on a deserted beach) practice charity, write poetry, are thrifty, practical and self-sufficient, modest in their needs with a minimum of personal possessions, and, in brief: "live the joyous life in America without much money." (161)

Japhy Ryder is the very epitome of the dharma bum archetype. He is a scholar, a poet, a serious and diligent practitioner of zen disciplines, a mountaineer, and a modern Thoreau, living in a modest shack ("twelve by twelve") with only the most essential furnishings. He is also another Kerouoacian incarnation of that hero of the American Dream: the self-made man. Consistent with that celebrated tradition he was (like Andrew Jackson and Abraham Lincoln) brought up in a log cabin in a remote backwoods environment. Japhy has worked in the woods as a logger, worked aboard merchant ships, and achieved distinction as an Oriental scholar, speaking both Chinese and

Japanese, and is widely read in Tibetan, Chinese, Japanese, Mahayana, Hinayana and Burmese Buddhist texts, as well as Chinese poetry.(12) His individualistic, original ideas and life-style are entirely of his own invention. Ray characterizes Japhy in terms of American heroic traditions: "His voice was deep and resonant and somehow brave, like the voice of oldtime American heroes and orators. Something earnest and strong and humanly hopeful ... a great new hero of American culture." (14, 32) Ray also compares Japhy to cowboy hero Buck Jones and to Natty Bumpo (58) frontiersman hero of James Fennimore Cooper's *The Leatherstocking Tales.*

In spite of the corruption of cities – "that city of ignorance which is the modern city" (113) – there is still solitude and salvation to be found in the American wilderness. Despite the "well-paid," ever-vigilant, ever-pestiferous police – cruising the streets "in brand new cars with all that expensive radio equipment" (121) or casting "a steely look through dark glasses" (159) – ensuring that no-one sleeps on a beach or in a grove of trees or hops a freight, and causing poor paranoid Rosie to take her own life in fear of "a big new revolution of the police," (110) Ray takes heart believing in an imminent revolution of tenderness that will redeem the Dream. The liberation toward which he and Japhy strive is a freedom beyond mere political freedom, it is a liberation from craving, false needs and ego. Both Ray and Japhy agree that the dharma bums represent a seed of sacred energy germinating in the oil-stained earth of industrial America. "Something will come of it," (71) Ray prophesies. And later Japhy concurs: "I *know* somethin good's gonna come out of all this!" (210) "Who knows," he adds, "the world might wake up and burst out into a beautiful flower of Dharma everywhere." (211) Notwithstanding the narrator's early caution to the reader that the story is told retrospectively and that he has since "become a little hypocritical about my lip-service and a little tired and cynical, "(5) the tone of *The Dharma Bums* is decidedly optimistic, celebrating "an America that is still magic America." (119)

Further evidence of a magic spirit abroad still in America is to be found in a short-story by Kerouac titled "The Rumbling, Rambling Blues." [32] The story features as its central character a variant representation of the dharma bum figure or religious wanderer: a nameless, old negro hobo, a man of sorrows and soul-wisdom. In *The Dharma Bums,* Ray approaches matters of the spirit and men and women of the spirit in an inclusive, eclectic manner. He considers as fellow dharma bums persons who do not overtly or consciously embrace Buddhism, figures such as "the little bum of Saint Teresa" (7) whom Ray encounters while riding a freight train, the African-American preacher lady whose spirited sermon in a park he admires, (113-14) and the Jewish ex-Marine bum he meets in the railroad yards of Los Angeles. (117-18) Whether they will or no (or even know) Ray believes that by virtue of their humility and unpresuming reverence they, too, turn the wheel of True Meaning or Dharma. In a similar manner, then, the weathered wise old hobo of "The Rumbling, Rambling Blues" is a spirit-teacher, a truth-preacher, an apostle of dharma. He shrewdly intuits the psychic predicament of Slim, the narrator (staticity, stagnation) and is able to redeem him from it, in effect, summoning Slim back to his true vocation as a wayfarer. "You's a river log ain't rollin," the old man pronounces, "CAUGHT in a snag." (43) Like the Old Man with the Word who haunts *On the Road* and brings Sal a clearer, if bleaker, understanding of life, the swamp-born, time-worn hobo sage of "The Rumbling, Rambling Blues" has about him a mythic, prophetic aura, and, like a seer, his words carry deeper resonances. A ragged, solitary prophet wandering "the ragged Promised Land," – "he walked the American night just as he was, the burlap pants, the rope, the tarpulin apron." (41) The presence in contemporary American society – amid television sets, shopping centers and shiny cars – of this peculiar potent "ghost" (44) of a man serves to confirm that magic and the mystical have not altogether fled, but yet endure in America in marginal, unconsidered districts somewhere beyond the well-lit city streets, in places where the dingy edges of cities can magically become thresholds into a wider life.

There is a form of enchantment – more a beguilement – to which many are susceptible that is in conflict with mystery and magic, a seductive enchantment that is both the counterfeit and antithesis of mystery and magic. This is the allure of the glittering, glamourous perquisites of material success: excitement, admiration, sophistication, sexual attraction, luxury. In *Maggie Cassidy*, Kerouac represents the conflict between the magic of what is true, deep and essential in life with the fascination of what is illusory, shallow and empty, tracing the journey of young Jacky Duluoz from his small town high school to New York city and back home again. [33] The novel combines Kerouac's anti-urban theme with the motif of the Faustian bargain.

The choice from the outset of the novel, when Jacky Duluoz is sixteen years old – still a boy among his boy gang of pals – is between a future life as Jack of Diamonds or as Jack of Hearts. He can either pursue his ambitions or follow his feelings for Maggie Cassidy, a local working class girl to whom he is powerfully attracted. A portent of the trap into which he will fall if he yields to his vanity and ambitions is the heavy athletic sweater he chooses to wear to his birthday party, knowing that his photograph will be taken and appear in the local paper, and he will be seen to be a letterman, a varsity athlete. The sweater proves to be for him a kind of personal purgatorial prison: "I'm sweating," he laments, "the big athletic sweater is killing me, making me hot, wetfaced, sad at my own party." (135) This symbolic warning notwithstanding though, he envisions for himself a future life of polish and poise, a celebrated athlete and pipe-smoking college scholar, an urbane reader of *The New York Times*, one for whom life's "special honors" are reserved. (143) No warning or omen can dissuade him from the pursuit of his vision of the American Dream of Success: "I was going to be a big hero of New York with rosy features and white teeth ... an incarnation of the American Super Dream Winner," living in a penthouse with "a wife beautiful beyond belief, not Maggie." (166-67)

Another portent of the deceptive nature of the shimmering promise young Jacky so ardently pursues in New York city can be seen in the huge milkshakes he buys on Times Square: "impossibly aerated like cotton you drank illusion of liquid like the taste of New York." (169) His dreams of upward mobility, elegance and urban glamour cost him, in the end, the love of Maggie Cassidy – associated with the trees and the river, the cottages and stars of quiet idyllic Lowell – who is repelled by the city of New York and its inhabitants. Maggie rightly forecasts Jacky's future: "you'll burn yourself out like a moth jumping into a locomotive boiler looking for light ... and lose yourself from yourself." (184) And that, in essence, is what occurs. At the end of the novel, set three years after his last meeting with Maggie, his dreams gone all awry, Jack is working as a garageman in his hometown and has become proud, predatory and "cold hearted." (194) The "diamonds" of his dreams failed to materialize but the heart nevertheless was forfeit. The magic of love has taken flight from his life. Literally and figuratively, when last we see him, he is left "skittering crazily in the slush." (194)

The wish that animates much of Kerouac's writing is for a world of sincerity, simplicity and innocence, as exemplified in the figure of Maggie Cassidy. The America Kerouac loves is that of Maggie Cassidy's modest, homely habitat, her family's wooden cottage near the river, with a porch and an apple tree, sunflowers and a swing, summer stars and fire flies. Maggie nurtures no grand ambitions; she desires only marriage and children, and a handsome husband who – like her father – works as a brakeman on the railroad and comes home for supper whistling down the street, bearing his brakeman's lantern through the evening to their cottage. Kerouac also loves the America of free-spirits like Japhy Ryder, working man and mountaineer, glad poet and happy scholar, thriving at the margins of American life, living without pretence and deceit, going his own way in the world. For Kerouac, unaffected, uncomplicated Maggie and independent, self-reliant Japhy (and eager, earnest, damaged Dean) testify to the persistence of "the essential and everlasting America."

The America Kerouac treats as unworthy, as hollow and devoid of meaning, is the America of material wealth and spiritual impoverishment, of outward success and status and acquisition, of televisions and appliances and all the impedimenta of consumer culture. By the same token, he disdains the pinched and paltry spirits of those who dedicate their lives to a single-minded pursuit of possessions and property, prestige and personal gain, and who cultivate self-interest at the price of self-actualization. There is, I think, a clear link between Kerouac and the anti-materialistic perspectives of Henry David Thoreau and Ralph Waldo Emerson. Parallels are many and striking between the Thoreau of *Walden* and the Japhy Ryder of *The Dharma Bums.* [34] And, I think, too, of Emerson deploring the competitive commercial world for its lack of "sentiments of love and heroism," and its prevailing ethos of "distrust, concealment, of superior keenness, not of giving but of taking advantage." [35] In the tradition of Thoreau and Emerson, the project implicit in Kerouac's writing is to reassess and repossess the American experience, to advance a counter-ideal, to propose an American community more whole and more human.

As noted above, in his writings Kerouac expresses strong critical reservations concerning law enforcement in the United States. Policemen are often seen by the author as overzealous, overbearing guardians of banal normality, enforcing codes and standards of acceptable behaviour that fundamentally derive from the interests of the mainstream culture. In two essays collected in *Lonesome Traveller,* a gathering of the author's essays and travel pieces, Kerouac elaborates upon this theme, contrasting ubiquitous and intrusive contemporary American law enforcement with heroic traditions of individualistic freedom in America and with the freedom of fellaheen cultures. [36]

In "Mexico Fellaheen," Kerouac juxtaposes the demeanour and behaviour of American border guards on the U.S. side of the border with Mexico at Nogales, Arizona, with the immediate sense of relief and freedom he experiences upon entering easygoing Mexico. The officers of the American border patrol are described by the author as "severe" and "sinister" in appearance and manner and annoyingly invasive in their suspicious searches of your belongings, whereas crossing into Mexico, the traveller experiences a rush of relaxation and a sense of freedom that the author compares to boyhood experiences of escaping from the oppressive presence of officious adults. In America, Kerouac complains, there are "endless policemen" enforcing "endless laws," (27) whereas in Mexico a casual, good-humoured, tolerant mood prevails: "this fellaheen feeling about life, that timeless gaiety of people not involved in the great cultural and civilisation issues." (27) In like manner, "The Vanishing American Hobo" contrasts the "footwalking freedom" once enjoyed by heroic American figures such as Jim Bridger, Johnny Appleseed, John Muir, Jack London and Vachel Lindsay, the liberty of movement and spirit celebrated in Walt Whitman's "Song of the Open Road," with the omnipresent "police surveillance" besetting contemporary America. There are police, Kerouac laments, on highways, sea shores, embankments, in railroad yards and dry river bottoms, all eager to press vagrancy charges on itinerant Americans innocently intent upon solitude or just staying outside of the social system. There are bored sheriffs patrolling lonely country roads aching to accost and arrest "the first human being they see walking." (155) It is this level of official control of independent citizens ("all I want is to be left alone" one drifter is quoted as saying on p. 154) together with the ascendancy of what Huck Finn called "sivilization," that has led to the near extinction of the storied American hobo, once an authentic American folk figure, now a pariah. There is, Kerouac warns, scarcely anywhere left in America for a hobo to seek seclusion, even in the woods, for, as he ruefully observes "The woods are full of wardens." (157)

Yet concurrent with expressions of displeasure and disapproval among the essays collected in *Lonesome Traveller*, there runs through Kerouac's autobiographical prose pieces a current of keen appreciation for the mysteries and splendours of America, "the real America" (12) of waterfronts and worn wooden piers with "lights ululating in the moving tide," (11) aged hotels of the far west where you feel "the warp and wood of old America,"

(40) radio broadcasts of distant "football games in Great America," (47) alleys, poolhalls, Chinatowns, Portuguese bars, freight trains, country towns with main streets of hardware stores, grain-and-feed stores and five-and-ten stores, farm lands with "sweetness of the fields unspeakable," (72) snowy peaks of the mountains, rivers and clouds, meadows of wild flowers, creeks and lakes, ravishing sunsets and starry night skies, and the exhilarating freedom of the open road. On balance, on the evidence of these essays, the things Kerouac that relishes in his homeland would seem to exceed in number and intensity and thus to outweigh those with which he finds fault.

A similarly celebratory course of thought and feeling informs Kerouac's "Introduction" to Robert Frank's photo book, *The Americans.* [37] In lauding Frank's visionary, innovative photographs, Kerouac writes a prose-poem of praise (not without some reservations) to the romance and sheer human wonder of the United States of America. He rhapsodizes over "the humor, the sadness, the EVERYTHING-ness" (ii) of the America that Frank has captured, both lonely roads and vacant landscapes and poignant, pregnant vignettes of city and small town life, Cleveland, Los Angeles, Chicago, Butte, Wasatch, Hoboken, New Mexico, Idaho, Texas, Kansas, Missouri, Florida: "what a poem this is." (iii) Kerouac hails Frank's stark and lyrical photographic depictions of American highways and jukeboxes, backyards and cars and gas stations, and all the innumerable particulars of American life, the peculiar poetry and diversity of the American people with every race and blend of humanity and every style and mode of being, the glamour and griefs, the sorrow and promise, the incomprehensible vastness and boundless variety and vitality of this prodigious and manifold land: "impossible-to-believe America." (ii)

A comparable level of ardour pervades much of *Desolation Angels*. [38] Through the voice of Jack Duluoz, Kerouac's thinly-disguised alter-ego protagonist and narrator, the natural beauty and the astonishing multiplicity and vibrancy of America are extolled. From the vantage of his Thoreauvian wilderness cabin or from the windows of a moving bus, Duluoz savours the scenes about him, the peaks and lakes, the pines and moonlit clouds, "the greenfields and orchards," (378) together with lonesome roadside diners and Chinese restaurants, race tracks and bearded Russian patriarchs on park benches, baseball games and football games and roaring bars and smoky, rowdy burlesque clubs. And jazz burning a blue streak through American life. Throughout the novel, Kerouac is effusive in his admiration of and affection for his country and even his countrymen. He refers to "my beloved America," (37) and expresses his gratitude for "free radio waves" and the "free wild youngtalk of America on the radio," (45) for freedom of movement and freedom from political persecution, and for the vastness of the land – " America so vast I love it so" (132) – and the indomitable spirit of its diverse and various people, who can never "be degraded to the low level of a slave nation." (46)

Such is his attachment to the country of his birth, that while abroad, in Tangier, Morocco and in France and England, Duluoz becomes afflicted with a powerful, intractable homesickness: "all I wanted somehow now was Wheaties by a pine breeze kitchen window in America." (347) In the midst of his foreign adventures, he dreams only of shouldering his rucksack and setting off "towards America, my home." (354) And, on his return voyage (third class) west across the Atlantic to New York city, he nearly weeps one morning to see floating among the waves an empty carton of Campbell's Pork and Beans, so poignantly does the sight of it call up in his mind the memory of his homeland.

As ever in Kerouac's writings, the author cherishes individualists and eccentrics, seeing in their refusal to accept generally accepted beliefs and behaviours precious human resources of independence and integrity in an age of mass media and consumerist homogeneity. Duluoz notes with approval the presence of endearing quirks and oddities among his poet friends and in a sidewalk newsvendor and among "the negro baggage-handlers of the Greyhound Company" (146) who dress so stylishly for their forays into the nightlife, and in the ebullient, irrepressible punster Harry Garden (father of Irwin Garden.) The figure who most compellingly embodies American individuality in *Desolation Angels* is the grizzled old Forest Service Ranger, Blacky Blake, "as profound a man as you'll find anywhere," in Duluoz' estimation, strong, erect, amiable, a consummate old-time outdoorsman with a maverick cast of mind. Blacky is scandalized to learn that his former Forest Service protégé, Jarry Wagner, has been blacklisted from government work by the FBI. "It seems like nowadays nobody can say anything any more the FBI'll investigate them," he says, adding "*Me* I'm gonna say my mind and I do say my mind." (86)

Once again, as in previous writings by the author, it is the authorities – the FBI, the bureaucrats of the Forest Service, the police – who represent to Kerouac an insidious meddlesome menace to American freedom and individuality. Duluoz silently berates the Forest Service for what he sees as their myriad interfering restrictions and regulations and for being a front for the lumber interests. (71) He takes exception to the power of the police to interrupt a peaceful (if inebriated) assembly of poets sitting on a curbstone (218) and he resents being surrounded by two squad cars and questioned by the police as he hikes out of Tucson and into the desert night to sleep under the stars. (249) He is disheartened and outraged when one early morning en route to a day's labour (bearing a shovel on his shoulder) he is fined half his day's wages for jaywalking across an empty street. "There are so many silly laws," (385) Duluoz grumbles to himself. A few pages before the conclusion of *Desolation Angels* the author rails to the reader against "the ogres of Law" in "Law Ridden America," and the "ten thousand cold eyed Materialistic officials" they serve. (393) It is significant that Duluoz never seeks to challenge authority but rather to evade it, desiring not to change the world but only to find within it for himself a space free of constaint. In this regard, he characterizes himself as "a man of contemplations" in the Taoist sense, aiming to avoid conflict with officialdom and its agents and "to see the world from the viewpoint of solitude and to meditate upon the world without being imbroglio'd in its actions ... I wanted to be a Man of Tao, who watches the clouds and lets history rage beneath." (248)

The "dreadful cities" (368) of America, long deplored by the author, are epitomized in *Desolation Angels* by Los Angeles which is depicted as an urban nightmare of hoodlums and drunks, junkies, whores and bums, "dirt and death." (377) And L.A. is seen by Duluoz as being far from unique among American metropolises. Misery and ugliness, hopelessness and sordidness are declared by the author to be identifying characteristics of cities across the nation: Cleveland, Washington D.C., Seattle, Minneapolis, Denver, Chicago, Philadelphia and elsewhere. "Whoever hath lived and suffered in America knows what I mean!" he exclaims in sorrow and anger. In the most prosperous, most technologically advanced nation in the world, in a land among whose most fundamental ideals is "the pursuit of happiness," how painful and shameful it is to find cities awash with human wreckage, with the flotsam of forsaken and forlorn lives adrift on tides of tears. His deep love of country notwithstanding, Kerouac remains keenly and sadly aware of the less favourable aspects of America, of the squalid nether realms to which some unhappy American lives are forever consigned. His hosannas are never unalloyed.

In *Big Sur*, Jack Duluoz himself descends into a squalid nether realm, not one of penury and deprivation, but an inward infernal region of acute distress and despair. [39] This wretched psychic state was prefigured in *Desolation Angels* where the protagonist-narrator experienced sudden depressive episodes in which his mind reeled with "bottomless horror" (71) Near the end of that novel, Duluoz relates sensations of seeing "Horror Everywhere" (391) and feeling himself "lost in unutterable mental glooms." (395) In *Big Sur*, such grim and dismal mental episodes become both more intense and more persistent. Although at the beginning of the novel, the harrowed Duluoz temporarily evades his depression and self-destructive behaviours, seeking refuge in a remote Thoreauvian cabin, finding restoration there in simple tasks and practical Thoreauvian thrift, a hopeless, hideous dejection and hallucinatory terror soon overtake him. One dire effect of this crisis of the mind and spirit is to isolate Duluoz from the sustenance he has always drawn from natural beauty – a central component of the narrator's and the author's attraction to the American continent. Indeed, natural features and phenomena are now experienced by Duluoz as fearful and sinister, as leprous and treacherous, as malign and malefic. Whereas previously in Kerouac's writings it was only cities that were depicted as sites of affliction, now both cities (San

Francisco is seen here as a trap) and pristine natural settings are equally realms of evil and suffering.

American society also evokes from Duluoz only rebuke and censure. Attempting in vain (and in physical pain) to hitchhike between Big Sur and the town of Monterey – his final experience on the American road – Duluoz is left pitifully rideless on the side of the road, as hundreds upon hundreds of bright, sleek cars filled with "witless," "sneering," (44) well-dressed, prosperous Americans insouciantly pass him by. Duluoz finds their fastidiousness and their shallowness contemptible. The lives of the American public are seen by him as lacking in originality, individuality and curiosity, and circumscribed by convention. "The P.T.A." he laments, "has prevailed" (45) over everyone. [40] Even Cody Pomeray – erstwhile irrepressible embodiment of the wild Western spirit – has been subdued and domesticated, now obliged either to deceive his wife or to ask her permission in order to whoop it up for an evening with his bohemian pals. A sad sense of aftermath or epilogue hangs over *Big Sur,* the remaining wide-open spaces of the American landscape are being encroached upon by ever-expanding suburban sprawl, families in station wagons and natty executives in shiny sedans have assumed possession of the open road, while time and misfortune have humbled those broken old heroes of the highway, Cody and Jack.

If the open road has reached a dead end, if the traveller can no longer fare forward, there remains then only one direction in which to move: backward – backward in the direction of the past, back to where the journey first began. In *Vanity of Duluoz,* the eponymous protagonist-narrator, now middle-aged, sedentary and subdued, takes a backward look at his early years, reviewing and reassessing from the perspective of the present the choices and events that determined his later life. [41] The subjects addressed in the author's book-long monologue include sports, love, ambition, war, America, and God. A tone of disillusionment is set already in the opening paragraphs of the novel, where the narrator addresses his wife, lamenting that "people have changed so much" since his youth, that "I don't recognize them as people any more or recognize myself as a real member of something called the human race." (3) Duluoz believes that a revolution in manners (or a revolution of the ill-mannered) has occurred in America, one precipitated in large measure by widespread ownership of automobiles, an insidious upheaval in attitudes and behaviour that has caused people in general to lose essential and once prevalent human values such as earnestness, purposefulness, poise, courtesy and simplicity. He soon extends his indictment of contemporary Americans to include mendacity – "everyone's begun to lie," (7) he says – and, at length, his disapproval expands to include a range of behaviours in American life that he finds objectionable: "what possible feeling can be left in me for an 'America' that has become such a potboiler of broken convictions, messes of rioting and fighting in the streets, hoodlumism, cynical administration of cities and states, suits and neckties the only feasible subject, grandeur all gone into the mosaic mesh of Television ... everybody dressed alike looking around at everybody ... only occasionally looking up at the trees." (97-98)

As in *Maggie Cassidy*, central to *Vanity of Duluoz* is the theme of the Dream of Success. Already as a boy, we are told, young Duluoz nourishes images of romantic possibility that he gleans from films: idealized fantasies of college and career and sophisticated city life – all remote from his small-town, working class origins. Looking back on his youth with rueful amusement, he admits: "I, of all things wanted to end up on a campus somewhere smoking a pipe, with a button down sweater, like Bing Crosby serenading a coed in the moonlight." (9) "The further dream," he recounts, "was to graduate from college and become a big insurance salesman wearing a gray felt hat getting off the train in Chicago with a briefcase and being embraced by a blond wife on the platform, in the smoke and soot of the bigcity hum and excitement." (10) His only path to such a life lies across the hundred yards of the football field, in his ability to leverage his skills at football into an athletic scholarship. "Making good" in life becomes for a time Duluoz' all-absorbing aim, to "make good" (23) to justify his father, to "make good" (24) for the sake of his mother, to excel and achieve for the sake of attaining his dream of personal success. And make good, he does, striving, studying, enduring gruelling football practices and brutal games, attending on an athletic scholarship first a posh prep school and then a prestigious university, becoming "the great American football player" (89) and the pipe-smoking, sweater-clad college student, vice-president of his college sophomore class. His aims, it would seem, are being achieved, his dreams already partly fulfilled.

Another ambition, however, another more urgent aim in life, suddenly overthrows in an instant Duluoz' long-cherished dream of success. Seized with the dream of becoming a writer, he abandons football and college and "in the most important decision of my life," (87) disappointing his parents and his coach, dives headlong into the raw life of the American road and workplace, becoming for the sake of his art "an American careener." (87) He travels, he works in factories, works construction, works in a garage, works as a sportswriter on a local paper, works as a merchant seaman, psychos out of the navy, lands in jail, reading, reading, writing, writing all the while. When after much toil and travail, Duluoz completes "1,183 pages" of a novel, (257) succeeds in placing the manuscript with a publisher, and the book appears in print, his pleasure is fleeting. "Nothing ever came of it," (257) he remarks. Literary fulfillment was elusive and illusory. His comment can be seen to connect with a similar pronouncement in the first paragraph of the novel, where the narrator characterizes himself as an author "whose very 'success,' far from being a happy triumph ... was the sign of doom Himself." (3) In brief, all of his ambitions in life, every goal he set for himself, every effort and endeavour, every labour and struggle – whether on the playing field, in the classroom or wrestling with words at the typewriter – was but a vanity: motivated by pride and lacking in true value.

From out of the collapse and ruin of his cherished dreams of success, though, a chastened Duluoz salvages other vital American dreams: the dream of personal freedom and the dream of self-actualization through spiritual growth. The ideal of self-reliance, independence and freedom in *Vanity of Duluoz* is embodied in the figure of Andrew Jackson Holmes, known as Big Slim, whom Duluoz meets while incarcerated in a naval mental hospital. Slim's given names associate him, of course, with heroic American traditions. Indeed, in his study of the American Dream, Jim Cullen portrays Andrew Jackson as a champion of the kind of roughcast, poor-but-proud Americans who were not, as Cullen says, inclined to defer to their so-called betters. [42] Slim is a downhome All-American hero, ex-football player, gambler, brawler, merchant seaman, hobo, oil rig roughneck and bronco busting cowboy. Duluoz admires him and recognizes in him an "independent and free-minded man," (150) whose physical vitality is matched by his spirited defiance of overweening authority. Big Slim is a kind of populist prophet, unyielding in his resistance to being exploited, imposed upon or diminished by systems, organizations or institutions; he is a figure akin to Jack Malloy in James Jones' novel, *From Here to Eternity*, R.P. McMurphy in Ken Kesey's *One Flew Over the Cuckoo's Nest*, Lucas Jackson in Donn Pearce's *Cool Hand Luke*, and a precursor (in the internal chronology of *The Duluoz Legend*) to the rambunctious Dean Moriarty. [43] Against the prying, tendentious questions of a military psychiatrist, Duluoz, like Big Slim, asserts his own defiant defense of the integrity of the individual mind, describing himself as "a man of independence," and an apostle of "independent thought." (154) Personal freedom remains for Kerouac an essential condition of authentic human life and the defense of personal freedom against all that is inimical to it an enduring concern in his writing.

Vanity of Duluoz also affirms, as I have noted above, the dream of spiritual unfolding and fulfillment. In the course of the novel, Duluoz ruminates on the nature of existence and the role of God in life on earth. He cites Blaise Pascal as exhorting humans to look to God for the cure to our misfortunes, placing our hope in salvation and a purified afterlife in heaven, but then admits his own inability to do so, remaining, instead, as he says, "entrap't in trembling weak flesh." (125) Later in the book, Duluoz ponders whether – in spite of suffering and tragedy – the image of God might yet be immanent in the world. Again, to elucidate his reflections on this question, he cites an argument made by Pascal: "There are perfections in Nature which demonstrate that She is the image of God, and imperfections to assure us that She is no more than His image." (163) To this formulation, Duluoz then gives his assent. Turning the same question in his mind once again still later in the novel, he first inclines to pronounce the created world cruel and heartless, the emanation of a God of Wrath, but then – building upon his earlier acceptance of Pascal's statement – relents, declaring: "we know that the brutish, the mean-hearted, the Mad Dog creation has a side of compassionate mercy in it ... we have seen the brutal creation send us the Son of Man, to prove that we should follow His example of mercy, brotherly love, charity, patience, gave Himself up without a murmur to be sacrificed." (253-54) Finally, as a personal proof of God's mercy and a sign of having at last attained – despite tormenting doubt and the turmoil of his life – a sustaining spiritual harbourage, there is Duluoz' vision of the cross: "I can't escape its mysterious penetration into all this brutality. I just simply SEE it all the time." (255) Whichever other ambitions and dreams in his life may have failed or proved to be mere vanities, Duluoz has been blessed in finding that which is pre-eminently precious, a truth of enduring worth. He has (at least in part) achieved the original American aspirational ideal, the earliest American Dream. [44]

A final road journey – from south to north and from east to west – across the American continent shapes the last written work from Kerouac's pen, the novel *Pic*. [45] Assembled from bits and pieces of earlier writings made consistent and compatible by the author's revisions, *Pic* is narrated by a young African-American boy named Pictorial Review Jackson, who speaks or writes the story (addressed to his grandfather) in Black Vernacular English. Pic is thus both a racialized outsider and a linguistic outsider in America, a country boy possessed of an innocent eye through which to see and assess America and its inhabitants. Whatever his marginal status in modern mechanized America, Pic shares many of the same dreams as his white countrymen: "the dream of the coast" (as Jim Cullen names it) which is a particular form of the draw of the Golden West and the dream of the Good Life, and the dream of a home. [46] Pic and his older brother Slim (whose nickname may be seen to link him with Big Slim in *Vanity of Duluoz*) set out to hitchhike from New York city to California because the mythic Golden State is seen as offering abundance, temperate weather, opportunity, possibility and pleasure: "All that sun, and all that land, and all that fruit, and cheap wine." (59) It is a place, Slim believes, where you need never wear a coat, nor heat your house, a *locus amoenus* or a kind of promised land at the western edge of the continent, a place to be "safe and sound by the Pacific Sea to set down and thank the Lord." (68) It is in California that Slim and his wife, together with Pic, hope to establish a new and permanent home for themselves far from the squalor and poverty of New York, a house on a hill, a home in which to spend their lives.

In common with previous writings by Kerouac, *Pic* implicitly celebrates the multiplicity and diversity of American life and lives. Beginning in impoverished, primitive rural North Carolina, the narrative moves to grimy, glittering New York City, then west across the country to California. Pic travels the highways of America through wilderness and among green fields and rivers, past the historic buildings of Washington, D.C., past junkyards and fuel storage tanks, traverses iron bridges spanning ancient rivers and skirts oily harbours, travels through factory smoke and through rain, across New Jersey and Pennsylvania, Nebraska, Iowa and Nevada, through small towns and smaller towns and roaring cities, reaching at last the California coast for a joyous reunion with Slim's wife and a new beginning in life. Along the way, he encounters hobos and street prophets, white children and black jazz musicians, truck drivers, Indians and a kindly Catholic priest. Although the novel makes reference to slavery and the civil war, to Jim Crow and the Mason-Dixon line, Pic and Slim experience among white Americans more friendliness, goodwill and generosity than racism.

Slim may be seen as another embodiment in Kerouac's writing of the self-made man, one who as an accomplished self-taught jazz musician has achieved self-actualization (if not prosperity) in the face of considerable disadvantage. Slim not only plays jazz music but jazzes the language, too, so to speak, juggling and jumbling words and ideas, history and fantasy in playfully subversive riffs: "retired hero of the Seventeenth Regimental Divisional Brigade of the Confederate Union 'at got hisself shot in the left side tibular tendon and got hisself stickpinned with a Gold Star Purple Honour of Congress medal and is now hunnerd years old in his libr'y up yonder writin the Immemoriam Memories ..." (28) In a similar manner, Pic's African-American rural dialect is rich with archaisms and images. Pic speaks of the interior of his grandfather's humble house as being "clean like an ear of old dry corn;" (3) the yellow setting moon is likened by him to "a scant banana," (24) a medley of adult voices conversing is compared to the babble of water in a creek, (29) and the flush of pleasure he perceives on the faces of an Irish congregation is described as being "pink as a shoat." (82) In this final novel, as in many earlier works by Kerouac, vitality and creativity and genuine joyous life in America are to be found among outsiders and marginalized people.

A final theme worth mentioning in this posthumous coda to Kerouac's body of writing is that of human compassion, benignity and sympathetic awareness as sufficient for salvation. On Times Square, Pic absorbs the sermon of a lay preacher promising that at the Second Coming of Christ there will be no harsh judgement and eternal punishment, but rather "everyone will be saved forever." (68) In the interim, before that glorious event occurs, the preacher enjoins the crowd – not to piety, prayer, repentance and penance – but merely to "live as best as you can and be hereinafter kind to one another." (68) Later, after having listened to the misfortunes related by the various drivers with whom Slim and Pic catch rides, Pic reflects that "It was awful all them stories you heard. But I had a feelin in my chest that ever'body was doin their best." (79) *Pic* is, perhaps, the most harmonious of Kerouac's works, a picaresque (no pun intended) adventure with little tension or trepidation generated by the plot, minimal social criticism (only by implication) a gentle, genial spirit and a happy resolution. Among all of the author's writings, *Pic* is, I think, the most indulgent and well-disposed toward America and Americans.

As the earth rotating on its spin axis is said to drift and wobble, so Kerouac's treatment of the theme of America – a kind of vertical axis in his writing – might be seen to fluctuate and veer somewhat from one position to another, shifting by degrees from time to time and from book to book, but – seen over time and taken as a whole, with due allowance made for nuance and ambivalence – maintaining balance. At this point, before taking a final look at aspects of that theme, I would like first to consider some of the affinities Kerouac's writing on America possesses with that of certain classic American authors and with some contemporaneous contexts in which the motif of America in Kerouac's work may be understood in a broader perspective.

Many of the essential attitudes and inferences that make up Kerouac's views on America as expressed in his writing have (as I have occasionally suggested in the foregoing) antecedents in esteemed canonical writers of the American Renaissance, writers such as Ralph Waldo Emerson, Henry David Thoreau and Walt

Whitman. Kerouac's mid-twentieth century notions concerning identity, conformity and integrity are clearly anticipated in Emerson's celebrated essay on "Self-Reliance." That "society everywhere is in conspiracy against the manhood of every one of its members," that "whoso would be a man must be a non-conformist," and that "Nothing is at last sacred but the integrity of your own mind," are Emersonian positions that Kerouac implicitly endorses in his writing. [47] Kerouac would likewise, I believe, nod approval to Thoreau's observation that it is the deep, dusty "ruts of conformity" that prevent us from seeing "the moonlight on the mountains," and to Thoreau's counsel: "Let everyone mind his own business and endeavour to be what he was made." [48] Similarly, Whitman's urgent monition to his fellow Americans to "Resist much, obey little," would, I think, be thought commendable advice by Kerouac, who would doubtless also applaud both Whitman's declaration "I exist as I am, that is enough," and the Good Gray Poet's denunciation of "inertia and fossilism" as marking "so large a part of human institutions." [49] There is also, I think, a certain kinship of spirit to be found between Kerouac and that impish, unliterary, literary mastermind, the rowdy father of American fiction, Mark Twain. I am thinking here, of course, of Twain's classic novel, *The Adventures of Huckleberry Finn* (1885) with its central theme of a quest for freedom, of which Alfred Kazin has written: "above all [*The Adventures of Huckleberry Finn*] is close to man's stubborn sense of freedom." Huck, Kazin writes, just wants "to be free, simply free ... not responsible to older people's conventions ... free from all those who would plan his life for him." [50] There is more than a touch of Huck to be seen in the figures of Dean Moriarty, Japhy Rider, Big Slim, Pic and other Kerouacian heroes, as well, of course, in Jack Duluoz himself. (Add to this mix of

American forebears, borrowings of Spenglerian historical pessimism combined with elements of romantic primitivism and blend in generous portions of Buddhism and Taoism.)

The disapproval of certain American societal norms – norms seen by Kerouac as harmful and undesirable – expressed in the author's work shares a good deal of conceptual terrain with other social critics of the American postwar era. I am not implying that Kerouac was well acquainted with the writings of these social critics but rather that as a sensitive observer of the life around him he was responding to the same moods and alterations in American life unfolding during the postwar period as those scholars who wrote contemporaneous sociological commentaries. David Riesman's *The Lonely Crowd,* for example, argued that America was becoming a society whose members were "outer-directed" (compliant, conformist) rather than "inner-directed" (thinking and acting according to an independent self-concept.) [51] Similarly,William F. Whyte's *The Organization Man,* described and decried what the author saw as a new behavioural trend among middle-class Americans employed by large corporations and living in the new suburbs: an urgent desire to fit in, to belong to a social group and a concomitant conformity to group values. [52] Vance Packard's study, *The Status Seekers,* "an exploration of class behaviour in America," directed attention to another consequence of postwar affluence, a new, intensified expression of traditional American upward mobility assuming the form of signalling – with prestige-enhancing possessions such as car and clothing, a high-end home and by other means – the achievement of higher social status, in this way bringing conspicuous consumption to new levels of wastefulness and fatuousness. [53] The title of Sloan Wilson's novel, *The Man in the Gray Flannel Suit,* served to popularize a phrase which became a metaphor for an anonymous executive employed by a faceless corporation, one compliantly dressed in the standard uniform for office workers, a conformist who has traded liberty for economic stability. [54] The image may have been something of a reductive cliché but one founded, nevertheless, upon sad realities. In Kerouac's writings – most particularly in *On the Road* and *The Dharma Bums* – the author attempts to suggest an alternative to what he perceives as the constrictive, unfulfilling lives led by many Americans, celebrating, instead, the pleasures of simplicity, friendship and freedom, and the authentic satisfactions to be found in the cultivation of spiritual beliefs and practices. In this sense, Kerouac's work may be seen to complement the observations of social critics and other commentators during the 1950s, his writings proposing a kind of corrective or counterweight to a drift in postwar American culture (after the deprivations of the Great Depression and the uncertainties and insecurities of World War II) toward complacency and materialism; his earnest, personal words set down in solitude and put forward in print with the implicit aim of inspiring a remodelling of certain norms and values embraced by the prevailing culture.

Recalling that there is no single, definitive American Dream but an abundance of different dreams pursued by a myriad of different Americans, and having traversed the contours of Kerouac's work, the reader will by this point have a clear sense of which American Dreams the author endorses and of which he disapproves. The particular expressions of the Dream affirmed in Kerouac's writing include, of course, that over-arching, foundational dream "the pursuit of happiness," as well as the dream of personal freedom, of independence and agency, the dream of self-reliance and self-actualization, the dream of personal transformation and the living out of religious ideals, and – according to Kerouac's own subjective understanding of the terms – the dream of the self-made man and the dream of success (in the sense of "doing well according to one's own standard," as Robert C. Hauhart has written in a citation given above, or in the sense that James Truslow Adams, also quoted above, originally described the American Dream as that of "a better, richer and happier life.") The American Dreams to which Kerouac is indifferent or unsympathetic include those most commonly (reductively) considered to be *the* American Dream: upward mobility, economic and social advancement, the acquisition of worldly goods and material wealth, the attainment of success in terms of prestige or property.

There is, however, a considerable difference between affirming an ideal and achieving it, a great gap between intention and fulfilment. The disparity between promise and performance is a criticism that has often been levelled at the United States, and we see similar complications enacted in the fate of that all-American boy, Jack Duluoz. Indeed, the course of Duluoz' life, as depicted through Kerouac's novels, recapitulates in microcosm the way in which ideals and desires (including those that inform the American endeavour) are arrested by the hard, unyielding nature of reality, are worn away by adversity, or may be badly wounded in ambush by an inward adversary. Duluoz' dreams of overtaking "IT," of achieving *nirvana*, of helping to precipitate "a rucksack revolution," of achieving a simple and serene life in the world, all end in failure. His dreams are, in large measure, undermined by his compulsive drinking – a dark, destructive impulse from within that overwhelms him. How poignant and how piteously symbolic it is that in *Big Sur* the psychic shelter that a beleagured Duluoz finds in a modest Thoreauvian cabin set amid a remote redwood forest is overthrown from within, the peaceful equilibrium he so desperately craves transformed by the poison of alcohol into nightmare horror. Sadly, *Big Sur* is an anti-*Walden,* the very inversion and negation of Thoreau's spiritual awakening. In *Vanity of Duluoz,* the now battered middle-aged spiritual quester has found religious faith but has become bitter and irascible. "I wanted to be a Man of Tao," Duluoz declared in *Desolation Angels,* "who watches the clouds and lets history rage beneath." (248) In the end, though, that is far from being the case. Like the America he once described as being "ragged" and "tumbledown," in the end, Duluoz might well be said to have himself become in spirit somewhat "ragged" and "tumbledown." Sustained by religious faith, though, he endures, unsteady but unfallen, a damaged man who once followed so passionately an American dream of freedom, extending it beyond the boundaries of the material world and toward the infinite.

Kerouac's writing constitutes both a critique and an appreciation of America. He tells us of grimy cities and pristine forests, sprawling suburbs and towering mountains, and "all that road going." And inhabiting the vastness of the land, he tells us, are not only "the millions and millions hustling forever for a buck among themselves," not only those sitting passively before television screens in evening living rooms "looking at the same thing and thinking the same thing," but mysterious solitary prophets like the Negro hobo wandering the American night, and humble, prayerful, lonely vagrants like the little bum of Saint Theresa; abroad in the land there is that "wild yea saying overburst of American joy," Dean Moriarty, and that "great new American hero" Japhy Ryder and his maverick mentor Blacky Blake, there is genius jazzman Lester Young and his disciple Slim, there is that free-spirited, headstrong rolling stone, Big

Slim, and innocent-eyed Pic – like an angel or a budding saint – looking out onto the world in pity and wonder. What final appraisal of his homeland might be inferred, then, from Kerouac's body of work? Ultimately, most readers will doubtless place emphasis on those phrases or passages that suit their own outlook. For my part, I believe that – on balance – Kerouac saw America as metaphorically "ragged" and "tumbledown" at times and in places, but still a "promised land," still "holy" to him. America seemed to him, I think, a bit rickety, so to speak, its lofty and honorable ideals and dreams a bit time-worn and weather-beaten, but withal – wear and tear notwithstanding – a land still sturdy in its ultimates, firmly fixed in place, and still a place of promise and possibility, hallowed still by human hope, and in spite of everything, "still magic America."

NOTES

---

[1] The untitled poem in which this phrase occurs appears as an epigraph to "Piers of the Homeless Night" in Jack Kerouac's *Lonesome Traveler* (New York: Grove Press, 1960) p. 1. It also appears on the back cover of Kerouac's *Scattered Poems* (San Francisco: City Lights, 1971.)

[2] *The American Dream: A Cultural History* by Lawence R. Samuel (Syracuse, New York: Syracuse University Press: 2012) pp. 4-5.

[3] *The American Dream: A Short History of an Idea that Shaped a Nation* by Jim Cullen (New York: Oxford University Press, 2003) p. 7.

[4] *American Literature and the Dream* by Frederick Ives Carpenter (New York: Philosophical Library, 1955) p. 3.

[5] *Facing Up to the American Dream: Race, Class and the Soul of the Nation* by Jennifer L. Hochschild (Princeton, New Jersey: Princeton University Press, 1995) p. 3.

[6] *The American Dream* by Robert H. Fossum and John K. Roth (Durham, England: British Association for American Studies, 1981) pp. 1-2.

[7] *Seeking the American Dream: A Sociological Inquiry* by Robert C. Hauhart (New York: Palgrave, 2016) p. 13.

[8] *The Epic of America* by James Truslow Adams (Boston: Little, Brown, 1931) p. xx of "Preface."

[9] *Vanity of Duluoz* by Jack Kerouac (New York: Coward-McCann, 1968.) Page references hereafter are to Penguin Books edition, London: 2001. The passage quoted here occurs on p. 69.

[10] *Atop an Underwood: Early Stories and Other Writings* by Jack Kerouac, ed. by Paul Marion (New York: Viking, 1999) pp. 113-15. 123-25.

[11] Letter to Bill Ryan from Jack Kerouac, 10 January 1943, *Jack Kerouac: Selected Letters 1940-1956,* ed. by Ann Charters (New York: Viking, 1995) p. 37.

---

[12] "America in the World" by Jack Kerouac, *The Unknown Kerouac,* ed. by Todd Tietchen (New York: The Library of America, 2016) pp. 7-10. Page references hereafter are to this edition.

[13] "A Couple of Facts Concerning Laws of Decadence" by Jack Kerouac, *The Unknown Kerouac,* pp. 13-15.

[14] See, for example, William Cowper (1731-1800) *"The Task"* (1785) and William Wordsworth (1770-1850) *"Preface to Lyrical Ballads"* (1802).

[15] *Windblown World* by Jack Kerouac, ed. by Douglas Brinkley (New York: Viking, 2004) pp. 146-47. Page references hereafter are to this edition.

[16] *Virgin Land: The American West as Symbol and Myth* by Henry Nash Smith (Cambridge, Massachusetts: Harvard University Press, 1970) p. 57. Page references hereafter are to this edition.

[17] *"Paleface and Redskin"* by Philip Rahv, *The Kenyon Review,* Vol. 1, No. 3 (Summer 1939) pp. 251-56.

[18] *The Town and the City* by Jack Kerouac (New York: Harcourt, Brace & Company, 1950). Page references hereafter are to this edition.

[19] *Visions of Cody* by Jack Kerouac (New York: Viking, 1973.) Page references hereafter are to Flamingo/Grafton edition (London: 1980.)

[20] *America the Beautiful,* lyrics by Katherine Lee Bates, music by Samuel A. Ward (1910.)

[21] *Kerouac* by Ann Charters (San Francisco: Straight Arrow Books, 1973.) Page references hereafter are to St. Martin's Press edition (New York: 1994.)

[22] William Frederick "Buffalo Bill" Cody (1846-1917) scout, author, showman, regarded by *Encyclopedia Brittanica* as having personified the excitement of the American frontier.

[23] *The American Spirit* by David M. Kennedy and Thomas A. Bailey, (Boston: Cengage, 2006) p. 592.

[24] *Walden* by Henry David Thoreau, originally published in 1854. Page reference here to *Walden,* New York: Random House, 1946, p. 9.

[25] *Book of Sketches* by Jack Kerouac (San Francisco: City Lights, 2006.) Page references hereafter are to this edition.

[26] *The Decline of the West* by Oswald Spengler, publication in English 1926 (Volume 1) and 1928 (Volume 2.) Original title *Der Untergang des Abendlandes.* Volume 1 published 1918, Volume 2 published 1922.

[27] *On the Road* by Jack Kerouac (New York: Viking, 1957.) Page references hereafter are to Penguin Great Books of the 20th Century edition ,London: 1999. *The Dharma Bums* by Jack Kerouac (New York: Viking, 1958.) Page references hereafter are to Penguin Books edition, London, 1986.

[28] *Sound and Symbol: Music in the External World* by Victor Zuckerkandl (trans. from German by Willard R. Trask) Vol. 1 (Princeton, N.J.: Princeton University Press, 1969) p. 371.

[29] *The Dharma Bums* by Jack Kerouac (New York: Viking, 1958.) Page references hereafter are to Penguin Books edition, London: 1976.

[30] *"Passage to India"* by Walt Whitman, first printed as a pamphlet in 1871, then annexed to a reissue of the 5th edition of *Leaves of Grass* (Washington, D.C. 1872.)

[31] *"A Brief Recognition of New England's Errand into the Wilderness"* sermon preached by Samuel Danforth in Boston on May 11, 1670.

[32] *"The Rumbling, Rambling Blues"* first appeared in *Playboy* vol. v, no. 1 (January 1958) and was later reprinted in *The Permanent Playboy,* ed. by Ray Russell (New York: Crown Publishers, 1959.) Subsequently collected in *Good Blonde and Others,* ed. by Don Allen (San Francisco: Gray Fox Press, 2001) pp. 40-44.

[33] *Maggie Cassidy* by Jack Kerouac (New York: Avon Books, 1959.) Page references hereafter are to Penguin Modern Classics edition, London: 2009.

[34] *Walden, or Life in the Woods* by Henry David Thoreau (Boston: Ticknor & Fields, 1854.)

[35] *"Man the Reformer: A Lecture Read Before the Mechanics' Apprentices' Library Association, Boston, January 25, 1841"* in *Essays and English Traits* (New York: P.F. Collier & Son Co. 1909) p. 48.

[36] *Lonesome Traveler* by Jack Kerouac (New York: McGraw-Hill, 1960.) Page references hereafter are to Flamingo Modern Classic edition, London, 1994.

[37] *The Americans* by Robert Frank (New York: Grove Press, 1959.) Page references hereafter are to this edition.

[38] *Desolation Angels* by Jack Kerouac (New York: Coward-McCann, 1965.) Page references hereafter are to Palladin Books edition, London, 1990.

[39] *Big Sur* by Jack Kerouac (New York: Farrar, Strauss & Cudahy, 1962.) Page references hereafter are to this edition.

[40] The P.T.A. or Parent Teacher Association is used here as a figure of speech connoting complacency, compliance, banality and conformity.

[41] *Vanity of Duluoz* by Jack Kerouac *op cit.*

[42] *The American Dream: A Short History of an Idea that Shaped a Nation* by Jim Cullen, p. 66.

[43] *From Here to Eternity* by James Jones (New York: Scribners, 1951), *One Flew Over the Cuckoo's Nest* by Ken Kesey (New York: Viking, 1962), *Cool Hand Luke* by Don Pearce (New York: Scribners, 1965.)

[44] "America is unique in the extent to which religious goals motivated her founding and formed her early spirit. … The earliest dream, was that of living out a fully Christian life," writes Frederick Sontag in his article *"The Religious Origins of the American Dream,"* in *The American Journal of Theology and Philosophy,* vol. 2, no. 2, May 1981, pp. 67-68.

[45] *Pic* by Jack Kerouac (New York: Grove Press, 1971.) Page references are to Quartet edition, London, 1974.

---

[46] *The American Dream: A Short History of an Idea that Shaped a Nation* by Jim Cullen, "The Dream of Home Ownership" pp. 133-158; "Dream of the Good Life: The Coast" pp. 159-184.

[47] *"Self-Reliance"* by Ralph Waldo Emerson in *The Essays of Ralph Waldo Emerson* (New York: Random House, 1944) p. 30.

[48] *Walden* by Henry David Thoreau, *op cit.* Page references to Modern Library edition, New York, 1946, p. 379, p. 382.

[49] *"To the States"* by Walt Whitman in *Leaves of Grass* (New York: American Library, 1954) p. 36. Citation from *"Song of Myself"* in *The Portable Walt Whitman,* ed. by Mark Van Doren (New York: Viking Press, 1945) p. 84; citation from *Democratic Vistas, ibid.* p. 416.

[50] *"The Realistic Novel"* by Alfred Kazin in *Paths of American Thought,* ed. by Arthur M. Schlesinger Jr. & Morton White (Boston: Houghton Mifflin Co. 1963) p. 246.

[51] *The Lonely Crowd* by David Riesman (New Haven: Yale University Press, 1950.)

[52] *The Organization Man* by William F. Whyte (New York: Simon & Schuster, 1956.)

[53] *The Status Seekers* by Vance Packard (New York: David Mackay, 1959.)

[54] *The Man in the Gray Flannel Suit* by Sloan Wilson (New York: Simon & Schuster, 1955.)

POETIC LICENCE:

The Crime and Hard Time of Gregory Corso, or A Portrait of the Poet as a Young Felon

"When in disgrace with fortune and men's eyes
I all alone beweep my outcast state.
And trouble deaf heaven with my bootless cries.
And look upon myself and curse my fate ..."
William Shakespeare
Sonnet 29

"If you believe you're a poet, then you're saved."
Gregory Corso

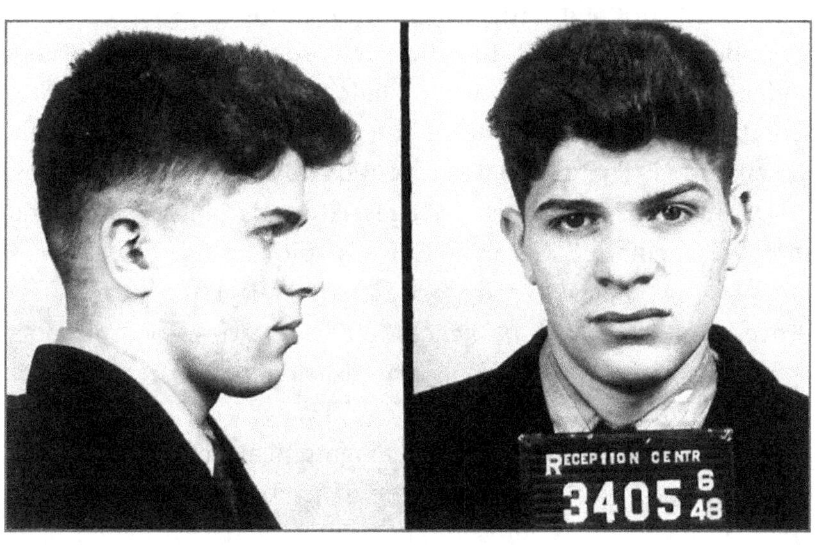

A plot to take over the city of New York, a cunning robbery with gang members co-ordinating their operation by means of portable two-way radios, thousands of dollars in loot, flight to Florida, living it up in the sun sporting a new zoot suit, betrayal by indiscreet and disloyal accomplices, arrest and a lengthy custodial sentence for having "placed crime on a scientific basis," incarceration in Clinton Prison at age 17 – in print and across the internet, myth and misinformation, inconsistencies and contradictory accounts regarding the circumstances of Gregory Corso's youthful crime and punishment are pervasive. Many of the falsehoods, it must be said, would seem to have originated with the poet himself. The origin of certain other errors and inaccuracies is unclear. To discover the true course of events, I contacted the New York State Archives in Albany, New York, asking their aid in researching court and prison records pertaining to Gregory Corso. The information on which I have based the following notes is a result of the kind help of personnel at the New York State Archives, to whom I am very grateful.

Before proceeding to official records of the actual events under discussion here, I would like to present a brief representative selection of some of the incorrect versions currently disseminated. That Corso was arrested and sent to Clinton prison in Dannemora, New York, at age sixteen is stated by several sources, including Carolyn Gaiser's pioneering piece in *A Casebook on the Beat*, "Gregory Corso: A Poet the Beat Way," Bruce Cook's *The Beat Generation*, obituaries for the poet appearing in *The Guardian, The Washington Post, The Los Angeles Times* and *The New York Times, The Dictionary of Literary Biography*, as well as in biographical sketches of Corso on the sites of *Poetry Foundation, The Academy of American Poets* and *The Harry Ransom Humanities Research Center*. The same claim is repeated in a piece titled "Seven Inmates Who've Passed Through Dannemora," appearing on the *NBC News* site, in *Gadfly* magazine, and in both *Who's Who in Twentieth Century World Poetry* and *The Continuum Encyclopedia of American Literature*. A French web magazine titled *L'autre* likewise avers that Corso was imprisoned from his sixteenth to his nineteenth year, while another French web magazine, *Salon-liternaute,* states that Corso began his prison sentence at the age of fourteen years. More commonly, Gregory Corso's age at the time of his arrest and subsequent incarceration is given as seventeen, as for example, in the *Encyclopedia Brittanica, Merriam-Webster's Encyclopedia of Literature, Modern American Poetry, 3a.m. Magazine,* on *Wikipedia* and elsewhere. Equally in dispute is the nature of young Corso's crime, with sources stating variously that he burgled a tailor shop (in order to secure a suit to wear on a date) or robbed a Household Finance office, either acting alone or as the mastermind of a walkie-talkie gang. Additionally, the nature of the merchandise taken in the burglary or the amount of money obtained in the robbery varies among sources, as do also the circumstances of Corso's arrest and his incarceration in Clinton Prison. [1]

As stated earlier, Gregory Corso is himself the source of much of the confusion surrounding his crime, arrest and sentencing, having at different times given dissimilar accounts of the events. Most famously, perhaps, there is the poet's dedication to *Gasoline,* his second volume of poems: "to the angels of Clinton Prison who, in my 17th year, handed me, from all the cells surrounding me, books of illumination." [2] There is, of course, a distinction between one's "17th year" and being 17 years of age, your 17th year begins immediately after your 16th birthday and ends when you have attained the age of 17. Most people, however, are unaware of this distinction and employ the expressions (17th year, 17 years old, age of 17) as meaning the same thing. Accordingly, it is somewhat unclear if in his dedication Corso means to indicate that he was 16 or 17 years of age. In a biographical note composed for *The New American Poetry 1945-1960,* Corso again writes that it was in his "17th year" that he committed an act of theft for which he was sentenced to three years in Clinton Prison. [3] In this regard, Corso told Carlolyn Gaiser that he was sixteen when the crime was committed. [4] In an interview with Robert King in 1977, Corso repeated that he was sixteen years old at the time of the robbery of the Household Finance office, and that he entered Clinton Prison at the age of sixteen and left at age twenty. [5] To complicate the confusion as to Corso's age at the time of his arrest and incarceration, in an interview with Gavin Selerie, Corso states that he "did three years" in Clinton Prison, "from the beginning of seventeen years old to the end of nineteen." [6] And further to that confusion, in personal letters collected in *An Accidental Autobiography,* Corso writes "at the age of 17 I went to prison for 3 years;" "came out twenty," and later writes of having "left prison at twenty." [7]

As to the commission of the crime itself, the amount of loot obtained, and the circumstances of Corso's flight and arrest, accounts of these are also at variance. Corso told Carolyn Gaiser that his walkie-talkie gang consisted of three: "each of the three boys took up an assigned position – one inside the store to be robbed, one outside on the street to watch for the police and a third, the master planner, in a small room nearby dictating the orders. According to Corso, he was in the small room dictating the orders when the police came." [8] When asked in an interview with Robert King to relate the circumstances of his youthful arrest, Corso replied that in the company of two other youths, he robbed a Household Finance office in New York city for the amount of 21 thousand dollars, fled alone to Florida, "bought a zoot suit," but was informed on by his accomplices and subsequently arrested, tried and sentenced. [9] Speaking to Gaven Selerie, Corso recounted much the same story, but stated that the amount of the haul was "twenty-six thousand dollars." [10] Corso has also remarked that the judge at his trial was unfavourably disposed to him for his use of technology (two-way radios) in the commission of a crime, having in this manner – in the view of the judge – put crime "on a scientific basis." [11] By way of contrast to these disparate accounts, an unattributed article titled "Biography of Gregory Corso" appearing on the *PoemHunter* website asserts that young Corso was sent to Clinton Prison for the far more modest crime of having broken into "a tailor shop and stolen an oversized suit to dress for a date." [12] This version of Corso's fateful felony offence is confirmed or echoed by David S. Wills in his piece "The Life of Gregory Corso," where Wills states that Corso was imprisoned "for stealing a suit." [13] Clearly, no single definitive version exists of any of the events, nor can a coherent account be inferred from the often contradictory information available.

The facts, then, as recorded on official forms of the State of New York Department of Correction, typewritten and signed, filed away these many years: the crime, conviction and incarceration of Nunzio Corso (for such was his given name and thus his legal name.) Nunzio Corso, alias "Sonny," was arrested on April 1, 1948 for the crime of Attempted Larceny, 2nd degree, committed on March 29, 1948. (Having been born on March 26, 1930, Corso was therefore eighteen years old at the time of the commission of the crime. Larceny in the 2nd degree is charged when the value of the stolen property exceeds a certain amount

of money; in the late 1940s this may have been 100 or perhaps 200 dollars.) More specifically, on 29 March 1948, Corso unlawfully entered an apartment, "via a key," and there stole "rings, a watch, a pencil, currency and clothing" to the value of 230 dollars. He had no accomplices, and upon arrest (only 2 days after the robbery) confessed to the crime, explaining that his motivation for the robbery was that he "needed clothes." Corso was held in jail until his trial on June 4, 1948, when at the Court of General Sessions, Judge Francis L. Valente sentenced him to be confined in a state institution under the jurisdiction of the Department of Correction for "a term of not less than two, nor more than three years." To be subtracted from this indefinite sentence were the 65 days that since the time of his arrest Nunzio had already spent in detention. This was, in fact, Corso's second felony conviction, the first having taken place when he was still a juvenile (13 years of age). He was then convicted on a charge of petty larceny for having stolen and sold a toaster. At that time, Corso was held in New York's municipal jail, the Manhattan House of Detention, known colloquially as "the Tombs" for its Egyptian Revival architectural style. His confinement there was for him harrowing.

After sentencing by Judge Valente, Corso was initially sent to the Elmira Correctional Facility located in Chemung County, New York, which serves as a reception centre tasked with the intake and classification of offenders. Nunzio arrived at the reception centre on June 10, 1948. Upon entrance, personal clothing and property were taken away from him to be sent to his father, Fortunato Corso. These consisted of a two piece suit and underwear, snapshots and an address book. At the reception centre he was also required to list those immediate relatives with whom he would be permitted to correspond or from whom he would be permitted to receive visits. While there is no record of any visits, Corso did on July 23, 1948 receive from his father a package, containing candy, playing cards, toothpaste, cigarettes, a pipe and pipe tobacco. A record of personal property later transferred from the reception centre to Corso at Clinton Prison includes the following items: 1 prayer book, 2 decks of playing cards, 2 letters, 5 books of matches, 2 tubes of tooth paste, 4 photos, 1 pipe, and 1 bar of soap. (Later, on November 8, 1948, from confinement at Clinton Prison, Nunzio would write a polite, neat, type-written letter to John Cain, the Chief Clerk of the Elmira Correctional Facility, inquiring as to the date set for a parole hearing and the status of certain personal belongings, "photos, snapshots, etc." which had not, he writes, accompanied him from the reception center to Clinton. On the photocopy of Corso's letter in my possession can be seen a handwritten note in pencil: "Inmate advised of parole date and given snapshots.")

After 82 days at the reception centre in Elmira, on 31 August 1948, through the tremendous gates of Clinton Prison at Dannemora, New York, passed the slim, slight, (5 feet, 7 inches, 128 pounds), young Nunzio Corso, to live his days and nights confined within those heavy walls. In an article published in the mid 1950s, titled "Inside Dannemora Prison," author Hal Burton notes that inmates of Clinton Prison have given it the ominous nickname of "Siberia." [14] Clinton Prison is, he states, "the bleakest, most boreal outpost of the New York State penal system ... remote and frosted in winter by roaring blizzards." [15] The institution is, Burton writes, "the very epitome of a felon's worst forebodings." [16] Similarly, in his book *Gates of Dannemora*, John L. Bonn writes of Clinton Prison as "this barred, narrowed place, enclosed within the gates of hell. The terrible hillside that they called the Big Yard, unspeakably ugly ...." [17]

Upon arrival at Clinton Prison, Corso was duly assigned a number (30129) and issued a coat, pants, shoes, socks, towels, cap, underwear, gloves and shirt. There are no further records of his presence there until March 3, 1949, when a report from the Warden and a report from the Principal Keeper were sent to the Parole Board prior to Corso's scheduled appearance before the board (to take place in July of that year). The report from the Warden states that: "He has not been reported for any infractions here to date. He is very young in his actions and he likes to fool around. It appears difficult for him to settle down either in his work or in his general behaviour. He is reported as being courteous, friendly and apparently resigned to his situation." A similar characterization of the young felon is furnished in the report of the Principal Keeper: "Corso has only a fair work record here so far. He likes to spar with other inmates and spend his time kidding and clowning. He shows ability to work but he requires considerable supervision to keep him occupied." A far more positive evaluation of Corso's behaviour is provided by the Warden in a letter to the Morrell Plastering Co. of New York, N.Y. (who had apparently written to the Warden concerning Corso's suitability as a future employee.) In his letter, dated November 2, 1949, the Warden writes: "His conduct since his incarceration has been excellent."

Nunzio appeared before the Parole Board on July 21, 1949. Their recommendation was that he be held until January of 1950. On January 19, 1950, he appeared again before the board. On that occasion, their disposition was that he could be released from custody either on February the 1st of that year or in July. Records

indicate that Corso received parole and was released from Clinton Prison on February 2, 1950. Upon release, he was provided with a ticket to New York City, a (one-time) state allowance of 20 dollars, plus 10 dollars and 85 cents in wages earned during his imprisonment. His parole expired on the 4th of April, 1951. He had, then, officially expiated his crime.

By his own account, Corso's incarceration at Clinton Prison was for him a formative and decisive event. He has written that it was in prison he discovered literature and realized his calling as a poet. In his essay, "Some of my beginning and what I feel right now," Corso states: "What would seem to most as a great injustice – being sent to prison in my seventeenth year, where I was the youngest inmate ... proved to be one of the greatest things that ever happened to me. ... In that time I read many great books and spoke to many amazing minds ... Sometimes hell is a good place – if it proves to one that because it exists, so must its opposite heaven, exist. And what was that heaven? Poetry." [18] In his "Biographical Note" in *The New American Poetry*, Corso named some of the books and authors he had encountered in his prison reading. These included Fyodor Dostoyevski's *The Brothers Karamazov*, Victor Hugo's *Les Misérables*, Stendhal's *The Red and the Black*, as well as works by the English poets Thomas Chatterton and Percy Bysshe Shelley, and the poet and playwright, Christopher Marlowe. [19] Elsewhere, Corso relates that while at Clinton Prison he devoured the 1905 *Standard Dictionary*, "every word ... all the archaic and obsolete words." [20]

Again, by his own account, in an interview, Corso states that while serving his sentence at Clinton Prison he was neither molested nor mistreated by the other inmates. This, he explains, was because he was Italian and "because I was young I had a kind of mascot status" among the Mafiosi. [21] In another interview, Corso elaborates on his status among the prison's powerful Mafiosi: "I was like a little mascot. That's where I learned to be funny in life. Because I made them laugh, I was protected. ... Man, their hearts were broken when I left prison. ... Prison food was really awful, but I had good food because the Mafia guys got the food from the outside. They cooked steaks and everything, and I was always invited to eat." [22] Strange to say, Corso also relates that it was in Clinton Prison that he learned to ski: "I learned to ski in prison. ... They had a ski lift going. I went down beautifully man, held myself right, and psshhh ...." [23] The incongruous presence of winter sports facilities in this austere, forbidding, maximum security prison is confirmed by Hal Burton in "Inside Dannemora Prison," where he writes that when temperatures at Clinton Prison plummet (sometimes to 40 below zero) "the winter sports season gets going full blast. There is a ski jump, a small bobsled run and a skating rink." [24]

Other incidents or circumstances – some given wide circulation – relating to Corso's time in Clinton Prison seem to me questionable or are clearly incorrect. One such widespread story is that while incarcerated at Clinton Prison, Corso occupied "the cell recently vacated by gangster "Lucky" Luciano." [25] This unsourced biographical item has been embellished further with details of a private phone and self-controlled lighting in the cell, and even further elaborated upon with claims that Corso's "cellmate was none other than mafia extraordinaire Lucky Luciano" [26] and that it was Luciano's personal library and personal "tutelage" that guided and inspired young Corso. [27] Charles "Lucky" Luciano was incarcerated at Clinton Prison from July 1936 until May 1942 (leaving Clinton more than six years before Corso's arrival). Luciano was in May of 1942 transferred to Great Meadow Prison in Comstock, N.Y. where he was to begin assistance to the Office of Naval Intelligence in operations advantageous to the U.S. war effort (for which services, following the war, Luciano's sentence was commuted and he was deported to Italy, the country of his birth.) [28] It seems improbable to me that Luciano's personal library would have included Shelley, Marlowe and Chatterton (more likely volumes by these authors or anthologies containing some of their work would have been available to Corso in the prison library) and it seems to me doubtful that any amenities that Lucky Luciano may have enjoyed in his cell would still be present and available to the fortunate occupant of Luciano's former cell six years later. I have been unable to locate a source for these contentions, only accounts that treat them as fact.

Another incident alleged to have happened to Corso during the early days of his confinement at Clinton Prison is that of his initial attempt to declare himself unaffiliated with any Mafia family, insisting, instead, that he was, "an independent," as he is said to have put it. However, according to this account (widely disseminated on the internet) in the prison shower room

Corso was subjected to an attempted rape from which he was saved only by the timely intervention of the powerful and

fearsome mafia *capo*, Richard Biello, who reputedly remarked: "You don't look so independent now, Corso." [29] Again, with regard to this story, I have been unable to locate a supporting source, only assertions that the event took place.

It is notable that the poets – Marlowe, Chatterton and Shelley – named by Corso as having catalyzed in him a realization of his own vocation as a poet, were all young rebels and heretics, proud outliers and prodigious inebriates of words. Thomas Chatterton (1752-1770), brilliant, reckless, rebel-poet was an impoverished outcast who died by his own hand before his eighteenth birthday, martyred by a materialistic society. Christopher Marlowe (1564-1593) was a shoemaker's son, immensely gifted, seditious, heretical, unruly, a tavern brawler, slain while still in his twenties in a drunken bar fight (or assassinated by order of Queen Elizabeth I.) And, Corso's particular poet hero, Percy Bysshe Shelley (1792-1822), wild iconoclast, ardent idealist, and passionate celebrator of love, liberty and beauty, was drowned aged 29 in the Gulf of Spezia during a violent storm. All of these writers are romantic paragons, all precocious, all prodigies, all unyieldingly defiant of the strictures and constraints of their era – social, political and literary – all sacrificial geniuses and doomed martyrs to the lofty cause of Poetry. It is not difficult to see why teenaged Nunzio Corso, orphan and felon, damaged and outcast, yet drawn to beauty and moved by human suffering, would feel affinity with and draw inspiration from such figures.

I am intrigued by certain of the items Corso took away with him from the robbery for which he was convicted. One of the items, it will be recalled, was "a watch." In an autobiographical article titled "The Times of the Watches," Corso has written of his early and intense fascination with watches:

"Throughout my childhood I'd do anything to get a watch." [30] In the article, he goes on to relate that the first thing he ever stole in his life was a watch, taken secretly from one of his foster fathers. When he first saw the watch, he writes, he was ravished by its beauty: "oh did my heart thrill, my breast beat, my brow sweat, my body itch. It was the most beautiful thing I ever saw." [31] Strangely, every watch he stole, bought or was given during his childhood was lost or stolen in its turn, the last of his watches being stolen from him while he was being held in the New York city jail prior to beginning his sentence at Clinton Prison. Although, clearly, a watch can be an item worth stealing for its cash value in a pawn shop or from a receiver of stolen goods, I wonder if Corso was not also tempted to take it for its irresistible beauty. The other curious item taken by Corso during the robbery in question was "a pencil." A pencil! Among the rings, currency and clothing (and, of course, the watch) a pencil. How incongruous. How singular. What motive, I ponder, might he have had in stealing a pencil? I like to see the stolen pencil as a portent, prophetic both of Corso's poetry and of his distinctive drawings, which have been compared to the drawings of Jean Cocteau for their "purity of line" and their "blend of the classical and the romantic." [32]

In view of the discrepancies between the actual circumstances of Corso's crime, his apprehension, his age at the time, and the poet's later versions of the same events, what may account for the various dissimilarities? A likely explanation can be found, I think, in an attempt by young Nunzio Corso to disguise from his fellow inmates the banal and bungling nature of his crime and capture. By inventing a more elaborate and dramatic scenario, he could hope to preserve a minimum of dignity and maintain some measure of respect among his fellow felons who might otherwise despise him as an inept amateur. Corso's later recasting of the actual events in response to interviews and in written biographical statements reflects, I believe, a psychologically necessary re-invention of himself. In the bleak midst of his misfortunes, he had – by way of personal salvation and out of ennobling aspiration – assumed the role of poet and so subsequently poeticized his crime and confinement, a species of self-mythologizing not uncommon among poets and artists. Corso may be said to have revised his personal history as a poet might revise a poem, thereby refining and enhancing it. In this way, his rather inglorious actual crime was transformed into one much more befitting a young poet.

I think, too, that the repeated claim by Corso that when sent to Clinton Prison he was in his "seventeenth year" rather than eighteen years of age, is not merely self-mythologizing but a poet employing the poetic device of hyperbole, an overstating for the sake of emphasis, in this case for the sake of poignancy. Corso's slight exaggeration of his youthfulness at the time of his imprisonment serves to convey more intensely, more effectively, the piteous forsakenness of his situation as felt by him during that time. Some of this pathos would be lost if his actual age were given. The poet's dedication of his collection *Gasoline* "to the angels of Clinton Prison who, in my 17th year, handed me, from all the cells surrounding me, books of illumination," is in itself a poem. In a minimum of words it evokes in the imagination of the reader a potent, multilayered, deeply engaging story that would have been much diminished by literal fact. Even the alliterative effect created by the repetition of unvoiced "s" sounds (seventeenth, cells, surrounding) would have been lost.

Nunzio, as I have noted, was Corso's baptismal and legal name. It was the name by which he was known to his father and brother and his many foster parents and to the authorities. He took the name of Gregory at his confirmation. That name had no official or legal status and was not used for any of the forms or documents pertaining to his trial, his incarceration in Clinton Prison or his parole. Gregory was a name he had chosen, selected from among numerous other possible names. In a similar manner, having chosen to be a poet, he chose to be identified by a new name, henceforth calling himself Gregory. We may say that in altering various prosaic facts to achieve a desired poetic effect, Gregory Corso was merely practicing the traditional alchemy of poetry, availing himself of the time-hallowed right of poets to exercise poetic licence.

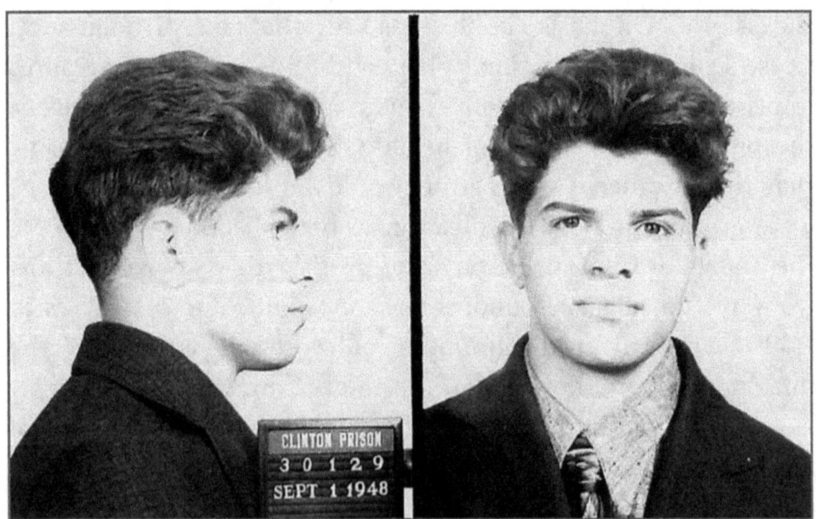

NOTES

---

[1] "Gregory Corso, A Poet the Beat Way" by Carolyn Gaiser in *A Casebook on the Beat*, ed. by Thomas Parkinson. New York: 1961, p. 268; *The Beat Generation* by Bruce Cook, New York: 1971, p. 134; *The Guardian* obituary, 20 January 2001; *New York Times* obituary, 19 January 2001; *Los Angeles Times* obituary, 19 January 2001; "Gregory Corso" by Marilyn Schwartz in *The Dictionary of Literary Biography,* Volume 16, Farmington Hills, MI: 1983, pp. 118-119; Poetry Foundation https://www.poetryfoundation.org/poets/gregory-corso; The Academy of American Poets https://www.poets.org/poetsorg/poet/gregory-corso; Harry Ransom Research Center http://norman.hrc.utexas.edu/fasearch/pdf/00190.pdf; NBC News, "Seven Inmates Who've Passed Through Dannemora" by Jon Schuppe, 8 June 2015 https://www.nbcnews.com/storyline/new-york-prison-escape/six-notorious-inmates-whove-passed-through-dannemora-prison-n371641; "Gregory Corso: Last of the Beats" by David Dalton, *Gadfly* 2001 http://www.gadflyonline.com/home/best_of_2001/THURSDAY-BOOK/BOOK-CORSO.html; *Who's Who in Twentieth-Century World Poetry* ed. by Mark Willhardt & Alan Michael Parker, London: 2000, pp. 69-70; *Continuum Encyclopedia of American Literature* ed. by Alfred Bendixen & Steven R. Serafin, London: 2003, p. 221; "Le Tempo Beat du Quatrieme Mousquetaire Gregory Corso" in *L'autre* https://www.lautrequotidien.fr/articles/2017/9/18/gregory-corso; "Gregory Corso" in *Salon-linternaute* http://salon-litteraire.linternaute.com/fr/c/search?q=gregory+corso; "Gregory Corso American Poet" *Encyclopedia Britannica* https://www.britannica.com/biography/Gregory-Corso; *Merriam-Webster Encyclopedia of Literature* ed. by Kathleen Kuiper, Springfield, Mass: 1995, p. 273; "Gregory Corso" *Modern American Poetry* http://www.modernamericanpoetry.org/poet/gregory-corso; "Gasoline – the imaginary & the pure" by Paul Stubbs, *3:AM Magazine* 11 March 2010 https://www.3ammagazine.com/3am/gasoline-the-imaginary-and-the-pure-gregory-corso/; "Gregory Corso" *Wikipedia* https://en.wikipedia.org/wiki/Gregory_Corso

[2] *Gasoline* by Gregory Corso, San Francisco: 1958, p. 3.

[3] *The New American Poetry* ed. by Donald M. Allen, New York: 1960, p. 429.

---

[4] Carolyn Gaiser, *op. cit.*

[5] *The Whole Shot: Collected Interviews with Gregory Corso*, ed. by Rick Schober, Arlington, MA: 2015, p. 104.

[6] *The Riverside Interviews: Gregory* Corso ed, by Gavin Selerie, London: 1982, p. 23.

[7] *An Accidental Autobiography: The Selected Letters of Gregory **Corso**,* ed. by Bill Morgan, New York, 2003, p. 122, p. 55, p. 19.

[8] Carolyn Gaiser, *op. cit.* pp. 268-69.

[9] *The Whole Shot, op. cit.*

[10] *The Riverside Interviews,* p. 22.

[11] See Gavin Selerie, Robert King et al.

[12] ”Gregory Corso Biography” *PoemHunter*
https://www.poemhunter.com/gregory-corso/biography/

[13] "The Life of Gregory Corso" by David S. Wills, *Beatdom* Volume 2, Dundee:2008, p. 49.

[14] "Inside Dannemora Prison" by Hal Burton, *The Saturday Evening Post,* December 29, 1956, p. 11.

[15] *Ibid.*

[16] *Ibid.*

[17] *Gates of Dannemora* by John L. Bonn, New York: 1951, p. 276.

[18] "Some of my beginning and what I feel right now" by Gregory Corso in *Contemporary American Poetry* ed. by Howard Nemerov, Voice of America Forum Lectures, 1965.

[19] *The New American Poetry op. cit.*

[20] *The Riverside Interviews, op. cit.*

[21] *Ibid.*

[22] *The Whole Shot,* p. 104.

[23] *Ibid.* pp. 104-05.

[24] "Inside Dannemora Prison," p. 67.

[25] See, for example, www.ndbooks.com/author/Gregory-corso, the Wikipedia entry on Gregory Corso, and myriad other online sites.

[26] https://untappedcities.com

[27] "Alumnus resurrects on the road journey of lesser Beat poet" by Josh Schonwald, The University of Chicago Chronicle, Vol. 28, No. 3, October 23, 2008. chronicle.uchicago.edu

[28] See *The Encyclopedia of American Prisons* by Carl Sifakis, N.Y. 2003; "Dannemora Gets Lucky" by Michael Berdan, *Adirondack Life,* August 2007, www.adirondacklifemag.com, "When Lucky was locked up" by Thomas Hunt, *The American Mafia: The History of Organized Crime in the United States,* mafiahistory.us/a004/f_prisonlucky.html, *The Mafia at War* by Tim Newark, N.Y. 2012, p. 269, 270-71; *The Luciano Story* by Sid Feder & Joachim Joesten, N.Y. 1994, p. 190.

[29] See *Wikipedia* and *PoemHunter op.cit* and "The Song of Gregory" colhernaboca.wordpress.com/2015/03; "Gregory Corso, um improvavel poeta beat" muralcultural2.blogspot.com/; "Gregory Corso: El angel de las Musas www.festivaldepoesiademedellin.org/es/Diario/Corso.html; "The Beat Poets of the Forever Generation: Gregory Corso" http.//the beat poetsoftheforevergenera.blogspot.com

[30] "The Times of the Watches" by Gregory Corso, **Cavalier,** December 1964, Vol. 14, No. 138, p. 36.

[31] *Ibid.* p. 92.

[32] *Beat Art* by Joseph Masheck, Butler Library, Columbia University, N.Y. 1977, p. 15.

BEFORE AND AFTER DESOLATION:
TWO SOJOURNS BY JACK KEROUAC AT THE HOTEL STEVENS

During the summer of 1956, Jack Kerouac stayed on two occasions at the Hotel Stevens in downtown Seattle. His first stay at the venerable old "skid row" hotel was in the latter part of June of that year, his second stay there some eighty days later in early September. Between these two brief stopovers, pivotal psychological and spiritual events took place in Kerouac's life, so that his separate sojourns at the Hotel Stevens stand positioned – like bookends – on either side of what was for Kerouac a crisis, a reversal and a reorientation.

Kerouac writes of the Hotel Stevens in two novels and mentions it in a personal letter. In *The Dharma Bums* (1958), writing as the narrator, Ray Smith, the author relates how having hitchhiked north from Corte Madera, California, he at arrives at length in Seattle, disembarking at the western terminus of the Bremerton/Seattle ferry: "I immediately went to a good clean skid row hotel, the Hotel Stevens, got a room for the night for a dollar seventy-five and had a hot tub bath and a good long sleep." [1]

In a letter to his friend Gary Snyder, Kerouac recounts how after a long journey north, reaching Seattle, he "got skid row room 15 foot ceiling and read VajChePraPar." [2] (Kerouac is referring here to the Vajracchedika Prajnaparmita Sutra or "The

Diamond Scripture," an ancient Buddhist text emphasizing the practices of non-abiding and non-attachment in attaining to a perfected way of seeing the nature of reality.) In *Desolation Angels* (1965), writing as the narrator, Jack Duluoz, Kerouac describes the Hotel Stevens in the following manner: "Hotel Stevens is an old clean hotel, you look in the big windows and see a clean tile floor and spittoons and old leather chairs and a clock talking and a silver-rimmed clerk in the cage – a dollar seventy-five for one night, steep for Skid Row, but no bed bugs, that's important." [3]

Staying at the Hotel Stevens for the first time, en route to his job with the Forest Service as a fire lookout atop Desolation Peak, then, Kerouac stayed in his room, piously studying sacred scriptures in anticipation of some form of illumination in the solitude of the mountain summit. This aspiration is expressed in a personal letter Kerouac wrote to his friend, Lucien Carr, on February 24, 1956, wherein he writes (jocularly but sincerely) of his hope that the seclusion and silence of the remote mountain peak will serve to catalyze in his mind and spirit a trans- formative, redemptive experience: "If I don't get a vision on Desolation Peak my name ain't Blake." [4] Returning to the Hotel Stevens eleven weeks after his initial stay there, having at this time just finished his assigned tour of duty on the mountaintop, Kerouac no longer devotes himself to the study of hallowed scriptures alone in his room but, instead, plunges eagerly into the whirling life of the world, hurling himself into a gyre of appetites and desires.

Midway between these two chronological co-ordinates, bracketed by Kerouac's separate sojourns at the Hotel Stevens, there lies a third point in time at which the author undergoes a kind of reverse conversion experience. In *Desolation Angels,* the author's alter ego, Jack Duluoz, recounts the slow erosion of his spiritual aspirations on the summit of Desolation Peak: "I'd thought, in June, hitch hiking up there to the Skagit Valley I northwest Washington for my fire lookout job `When I get to the top of Desolation Peak ... I will come face to face with God or Tathagata and find out once and for all what is the meaning of all this existence and suffering and going to and fro in vain´ but instead I'd come face to face with myself, no liquor, no drugs, no chance of faking it but face to face with ole Hateful Duluoz Me and many's the time I thought I'd die, suspire of boredom, or jump off the mountain." [5] Instead of the clarity to which he hoped to attain, the author experiences confusion, as expressed in the 6th Chorus of his poem "Desolation Blues:" "I just don't / Dont / Understand / I don't -- / I want to know / .../ I don't understand." [6] In the 7th chorus of "Desolation Blues," Kerouac admits that he now wants to forsake his solitary, ascetic existence on Desolation Peak, forsake his earnest, determined quest for illumination and salvation, and, instead, return to the world below with its cities and streets, return to wine, to delectable foods and sweets, to drugs and women and all the exciting, satisfying sensual indulgences available in the material world. As John Suiter observes in *Poets on the Peaks:* "Without the stimulation of a visceral 'Desolation satori,' Jack's longing for the realm of the senses grew ever more acute." [7] Or, as Philip Connors, a sympathetic fellow fire-lookout who once hand-copied Kerouac's Desolation Peak diary, comments: "For Kerouac the path of Buddhism proved too difficult, too alien to his temperament." [8]

HOTEL STEVENS, SEATTLE, WASHINGTON.

In consequence of his disappointment at having failed to receive a revelation of some kind on Desolation Peak, the author turns inwardly and then physically from the mountaintop (his idealized former objective) to "the valleys" and "the flatlands" below (see 5th Chorus of "Desolation Blues"). In more than one sense, then, at length he descends the mountain and seeks solace in what the King James Bible calls "the cities of the plain." [9] The Kerouac narrator may now be through with the mountain, but the mountain – as it were – is not yet through with him. This first becomes evident when Duluoz / Kerouac reaches Seattle and the temporary sanctuary of the Hotel Stevens.

In the mid 1950s, at the time of Kerouac's two stays at the Hotel Stevens, the old establishment – built on the corner of First Avenue and Marion in the 1890s – was long past its glory days and had become, as the author describes it, a somewhat shabby "skid row" hotel. The Stevens was exactly the kind of hotel that Kerouac cherished, not only because it was cheap and clean, but also because of its connection to the wild pioneer past of the northwest. A lingering link to the frontier past can be seen in the presence of spittoons in the lobby of the Hotel Stevens, as noted in Kerouac's description of the hotel (above) in *Desolation Angels*. In the 1950s remnants of the late frontier could still be found across the western states in the form of old buildings and other artifacts. (See, for example, the decrepit hotels and broken-down barbershops of Neal Cassady's childhood in and around Larimer Street in Denver as described in *The First Third*, and Kerouac's fascination with the weatherbeaten shacks and barns and gloomy poolhalls of the old west, as recorded in his *Book of Sketches*.) [10] And, as if in anticipation of the pilgrim's dis-heartened, life-hungry return from his mountain hermitage, in the street below Kerouac's room at the Hotel Stevens are to be found all the excitements and enticements of a big city night: the bright stores and lively crowds, the roaring bars, the wafting food smells of restaurants, and an oldtime burlesque theatre.

All of these attractions are eagerly sampled and savoured by Kerouac during the course of his post-Desolation sojourn at the Stevens. Afoot and alert in the streets of the city, Kerouac

immerses his senses in all the things of which they have been so long deprived on Desolation Peak. His unaccustomed eyes marvel to see the myriad and variety of lives in the world: "humanity hep and weird wandering on the evening sidewalk amazing me outa my eyeballs." [11] He humbly admits that for all his days of praying and pacing alone atop the mountain, the unspoken prayers of those he sees in the streets are as valid as his meditations and invocations, and he perceives that in each human heart there is latent love. He enjoys a cold beer in a crowded downtown bar, watching a prize fight on tele-

vision with the other customers, feeling a kinship with them and with others across America. Later, alone in his room at the Hotel Stevens, Kerouac drinks port wine, while reading, not the Vajracchedika Prajnaparmita Sutra, but *Time* magazine and *The Sporting News*, reintegrating himself in the affairs and events of the world. Returning then to the evening streets, Kerouac surreptitiously swigs his fortified wine from a plastic canteen he's filled as he relishes the pageant of the phenomenal world with all its diverse sights and sounds, recognizing how intensely he loves the world. High on wine, he attends a burlesque show, grooving to the jazz accompaniment, lusting for the dancers, all while becoming increasingly intoxicated on his secret canteen of wine. His excursion into the domain of the senses is crowned with a delicious Chinese dinner followed by a hot tub bath and long soothing sleep in a soft bed at the Hotel Stevens.

The critic and scholar, Jim Jones, has identified the burlesque venue at which Kerouac attended striptease shows in September 1956 as The Rivoli Theater, a conclusion in which author, Tim Appelo, concurs. [12] The Rivoli was located on First

Avenue only a few steps from the entrance to the Hotel Stevens and like the Stevens, was a remnant of an earlier era, having been built in 1913. Accomplished local organists such as Eddie Zollman and Wally Stevenson played the 2/5 Kimball pipe organ for strip shows at the Rivoli, and one or the other of these musicians may have been the organist so admired for his jazz skills by Kerouac in *Desolation Angels*. By the 1960s, the Rivoli had become a porn theatre. The building was demolished in 1970 (as was also the Hotel Stevens) and replaced by the Henry Jackson Federal Building, a 37 story skyscraper. The fate of the Hotel Stevens and the Rivoli Theater seems poignantly symbolic of the final eradication of the last traces of a certain rowdy, wide-open frontier spirit – a spirit celebrated in Kerouac's writing – and its replacement by a bland, slick and soulless new era. But, that all is in a state of flux, all fleeting and fugitive, would have come to Kerouac as no surprise.

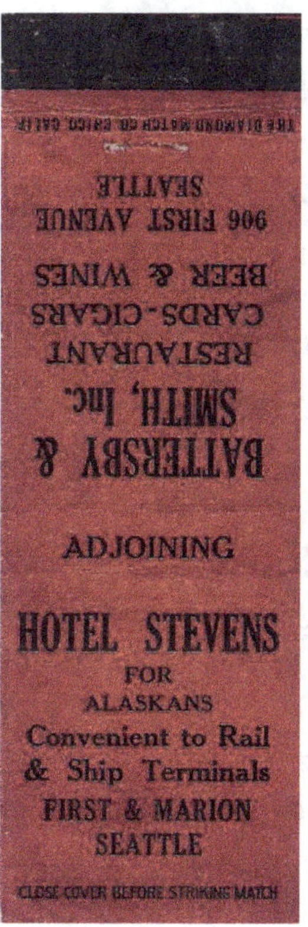

In the wake of his failed mountain vigil, Kerouac strives to reconcile his conflicting desires for spiritual attainment and for self-gratification, struggling to order his life in the world in a manner consistent with his ideals and beliefs. Preoccupied while on Desolation Peak with images of future sensuous enjoyment, Kerouac now finds that, having at last reached "the flatlands" for which he yearned and there indulged his appetites for sensation and intoxication, he is persistently haunted by thoughts and perceptions of a spiritual nature and even by a longing for his recent life of solitude atop Desolation Peak. On the sidewalks of Seattle, in the bar, alone in his room at the hotel, Kerouac cannot evade an awareness – engendered by his Buddhist beliefs – that all that he perceives exists ephemerally in "the unlimited void ... in the mind of the universe," and that ultimately nothing possesses reality or being apart from "mindmatter essence primordial." [13] Later that same evening, even during the most erotic moments of the burlesque performance, the author is uncomfortably conscious of a deeper level of reality underlying all things: "I see files of sorrowing humanity wailing by candlelight and Jesus on the Cross and Buddha sitting beneath the Bo Tree and Mohammed in a cave ...." [14] Drunk, dizzy, lonely and bewildered by the world, Kerouac remembers wistfully the mountain hermitage he so recently left: "I better go back to my rock." [15]

Kerouac's evening of diversion and immersion in the

pleasures of the senses culminates in an insight clearly related to his solitary studies and meditations on Desolation Peak. Leaving the burlesque theatre and standing on the sidewalk in the night air, returned abruptly from a realm of erotic illusion to gray reality, he sees two male performers and the organist from the burlesque house, scurrying up the street in an effort to get back to the theatre in time for the next performance. In an instant, the stage personae created by the entertainers and Kerouac's fantasies concerning the musician (as smooth, seductive lover of one of the strippers) collapse, as he sees the three men as "ordinary ... as *troupers,* vaudevillians, sad, sad – making a living in the dark sad earth." [16] This perception causes him to reflect that we are all mortals, transient, passing, and that all of us and all that we behold will one day vanish, even the heavens will disappear. The burlesque show may thus be seen as an implicit metaphor for the Buddhist concept of *maya:* just a show, an illusion of reality, a flimsy surface actuality, but ultimately in-substantial, unreal, uneternal.

In a similar fashion, Kerouac's separate stays at the Hotel Stevens can be seen to reflect his inner division: his sincere pursuit of spiritual growth in opposition to the powerful attraction of the pleasures of the senses. This conflict – between the spirit and the flesh – is central not only to Kerouac's life and writing but is, of course, a perennial theme in literature and, indeed, an abiding aspect of the human condition. The Desolation episode, flanked on either side by sojourns at the Hotel Stevens, is pivotal in *The Duluoz Legend,* as it also proved to be in the life of the author. Ahead for the author-narrator lay other rooms, further nights, days and distances, further ordeals and epiphanies. Having accommodated Kerouac with two night's lodging – first as antechamber and then as terminus – the Hotel Stevens was for this lonesome traveler a critical way station on his journey through the world.

NOTES

[1] *The Dharma Bums* by Jack Kerouac, New York: 1958, p. 221.

[2] "Jack's Haiku Letter to Gary," *The New Black Bart Poetry Society,* https://thenewblackbartpoetrysociety.wordpress.com/ .

[3] *Desolation Angels* by Jack Kerouac, New York: Coward-McCann, 1965, p. 105.

[4] Letter from Jack Kerouac to Lucien Carr in *Selected Letters 1940-1956,* ed. by Ann Charters, New York: Viking, 1995, p. 564.

[5] *Desolation Angels,* p. 4.

[6] "Desolation Blues" in *Book of Blues* by Jack Kerouac, New York: Penguin, 1995, p. 122.

[7] *Poets on the Peaks* by John Suiter, Washington, District of Columbia: 2002, p. 223.

[8] *Fire Season* by Philip Connors, London: Pan Books, 2011, pp. 190-191.

[9] *Genesis* 19:29, *King James Version.*

[10] *The First Third* by Neal Cassady, San Francisco: City Lights Books, 1971. *Book of Sketches* by Jack Kerouac, London: Penguin Books, 2006.

[11] *Desolation Angels,* pp, 101-102.

[12] *Kerouac in Seattle* by Jim Jones, Salt Lake City: Elik Press, 2004, p. 20. "Beneath the Cloudmopped Skies" by Tim Appelo, *City Arts Magazine,* October 28, 2009, https://www.cityartsmagazine.com.

[13] *Desolation Angels,* p. 103. See also "Seattle Burlesque" by Jack Kerouac in *Evergreen Review,* Vol. 1, No. 4, 1957, pp. 106-112.

[14] *Ibid.* pp. 109-110.

[15] *Ibid.* p. 110.

[16] *Ibid.* pp. 110-111.

MUTINOUS JESTER
THE COLLAGE NOVELS OF AKBAR DEL PIOMBO

Norman Rubington, a.k.a. Akbar del Piombo.
Photo by Frank Monaco, courtesy of Earl Rubington

Akbar del Piombo – illustrious subterranean luminary, mysterious, pseudonymous author of six darkly comic, wildly satirical collage novels. Akbar del Piombo – preposterous, portentous name, once widely believed to be a nom-de-plume of William S. Burroughs. Akbar del Piombo – the name itself a kind of collage, fittingly inconsonant for a virtuoso of the incongruous.

Concealed behind the Akbar del Piombo penname were the mordant eye and fertile brain of Norman Rubington (1921-1991.) Rubington was an acclaimed American artist – painter, sculptor, illustrator and filmmaker – who lived much of his adult life abroad, chiefly in Paris and Rome. Born in New Haven, Connecticut, he later studied at the Yale School of Fine Arts. During World War II, he served for three years in the U.S. Army, stationed in China. Moving to Paris in 1946, he supported himself there on the G.I. Bill and by writing pornographic novels for the Olympia Press. [1] It was in this latter capacity that he assumed the exotic nom-de-plume of Akbar del Piombo, subsequently choosing to publish his collage novels under that same ill-famed, fabled name.

Rubington's collage novels were clearly inspired by those of Max Ernst (1891-1976) whose original and important works in this genre include *La Femme 100 Tetes* (1929), *Reve d'une petite fille qui voulait entrer au Carmel* (1930) and *Une Semaine de Bonté* (1934). Carefully clipping images from 19th century and early 20th century steel-engravings, Ernst reassembled them in incongruous combinations creating fantastical, unsettling pictures that were then arranged in sequence and gathered together as a volume, forming a dream-like narrative. Ernst's collage novels sometimes included brief texts or captions, related only obliquely to the situations depicted in the images. Using source materials and methods similar to those used by Ernst to fashion his own collages, Rubington brought vital innovations to the collage novels he devised. These included the addition of extended prose texts recounting a series of linked incidents related (often ironically) to the collage illustrations, the use of word balloons in the collages, the arrangement of collages in multiple panel sequence, the technique of dislocating and recontextualizing unretouched original images (as I shall explain later) and the expression of more explicit, more topical satirical themes. Rubington's collage novels can thus be seen as among the precursors to the modern graphic novel, and with their futuristic settings and alternate versions of reality, can also be seen as a species of speculative fiction.[2]

The first of the Akbar del Piombo collage novels – and probably the best known of the six – is *Fuzz Against Junk* (1959). First published by the Olympia Press in Paris, the book was then marketed in the U.S. by the Citadel Press, later reprinted by New English Library and by Beach Books, and subsequently serialized in the pages of *Rolling Stone* magazine.[3] Subtitled "The Saga of the Narcotics Brigade," the novel recounts the exploits of Sir Edwin Fuzz, "foremost narcotics expert of the United Kingdom and sleuth par excellence," who is summoned to New York City to aid in combating an unparalleled outbreak of criminality there, the consequence of an equally unprecedented epidemic of heroin addiction. The prime mover of the burgeoning rate of drug addiction and its attendant wave of violent crime is an elusive figure known as "The Man," a criminal genius and a master of disguise. On the basis of the evidence presented to him by New York police, Sir Edwin shrewdly concludes that the true epicentre of the mayhem besetting the city of New York lies at the other end of the continent in San Francisco. Sir Edwin then leads a band of detectives to San Francisco where they disguise themselves as "beatniks," infiltrate the drug milieu of that city, and ultimately succeed in capturing "The Man," who, faced with imprisonment for his multitudinous misdeeds, chooses, instead, to commit suicide.

Although certain of the illustrations in *Fuzz Against Junk* have been modified by Rubington, the main technique employed here is one in which the original steel engravings are decontextualized and recontextualized. The intrinsic meaning of the images is radically (and comically) altered by dislocating them from the texts (crime and mystery stories, scientific journals, catalogs) they were originally intended to supplement and completely changing the contextual relationship in which they are now to be viewed. Placed in the service of a new frame of reference, as created by the verbal portion of the novel, the illustrations become humorously incongruous, absurd in their dissonance with the written words and with the reader's own wonted conception of reality. We see this, for example, where engraved illustrations of mechanical inventions, industrial machinery and medical or dental procedures are said by the narrator to be tools and techniques employed by heroin addicts.

The narrator himself – moralistic, credulous, and highly partisan – is another comic device deployed by the author in *Fuzz Against Junk*. Combining elevated diction with boyish enthusiasm, the anonymous narrator is the very quintessence of a "square," an embodiment of all that is conventional, unquestioning, prosaic and pedestrian. His callow commentary ascends to fervent adulation of Sir Edwin Fuzz and the police and descends to indignant vilification of the criminal and subcultural elements whom the forces of law and order oppose. Insensible to his conspicuous lack of nuance or sophistication, the narrator views with undisguised repugnance the "licentious" indulgences, "obscene" literature, "degraded" practices and altogether "brutish" behaviour of "junkies" and "beatniks," while the hip reader (the audience at whom the book is, of course, aimed) derives wry amusement from the narrator's zealous naiveté, so at variance with the hipster's own orientation.

In this regard, much of the book's satire is aimed at the square world's reductive caricatures of the drug subculture and the Beat Generation. Junkies are seen by the police as devious degenerates while beatniks are disdained as their depraved accomplices. Briefing his detectives in how to assume their disguises as Beats, Sir Edwin Fuzz instructs them to " bone up on Zen, refrain from washing and let your hair grow ... become adept in the Bongo drum ... familiarize yourselves with the Beat vocabulary." And, he adds – further to perfect their impersonations – in order to compose Beat poetry they need only "extract passages from the *Farmer's Almanac* and inject obscene words in the right places."

Humorous exaggeration is also central to *Fuzz Against Junk*, which depicts a world in which extremes and excesses, manias and obsessions are rife and the outlandish is the norm. An overdose of heroin causes a corpse to swell to gigantic proportions; in their insatiable pursuit of euphoria junkies employ "auricular injections," "oral incisions," "osmotic palpitators," "intra-cranium absorption" and opium vapour baths; equipment transported overland from New York to San Francisco by Sir Edwin Fuzz and his detectives to aid in their investigations of "The Man," includes half-a-dozen batteries of cannon; while detectives in San Francisco resentful of their interloping New York colleagues arm themselves against them with halberds. In common with the book's disorienting illustrations and equivocal narration, the device of humorous hyperbole effects a disruption of habitual perspectives and perceptions, causing tensile fracturing along safe certainties.

Authority and conformity, credulity and vanity are the targets of satirical humor in the second of the Akbar del Piombo collage novels, *The Hero Maker*.[4] The novel is set in a dystopian society that has displaced Eros with Thanatos, a society so deeply imbued with a distorted version of the heroic ideal that all of its male citizens nourish no other ambition in life than that of dying heroically. In this community, the Royal Heroic Society is a hallowed institution that – after deliberation by a jury – awards to aspirants the highly coveted official heroic status. This supreme mark of achievement, regarded as conferring immortality on the recipient, can only be granted posthumously, heroism being seen by its very nature to require the decease of the individual (in an heroic manner, of course.) The obvious irony here is that what is regarded as immortality – in the form of a statue or monument or merely an official certificate – necessitates personal annihilation, the untimely sacrifice utterly and forever of all ones potentials and possibilities. A further irony can be seen in the mindless eagerness with which multitudes of young men submit themselves to the various painful preliminary tests and the annual final (fatal) trial and in the agonies of ignominy suffered by the failed candidates for immortality.

While, clearly, at one level, the satire in *The Hero Maker* is aimed at the type of mass-based, militarist-authoritarian ideals that helped to generate two terrible world wars and numerous smaller conflicts in the twentieth century, at a deeper level the book is a critique of the blind submission to culturally inculcated beliefs and values that characterizes the general populace of all societies, large or small, and the competitive conceit that drives individuals to achieve the approbation of their peers and superiors. Gullible, lemming-like, against all common sense and every instinct of self-preservation, the determined aspirants to official immortality rush to their destruction. In a perverse variation of Thorstein Veblen's notion of conspicuous consumption, in *The Hero Maker* the price of achieving social prestige is conspicuous self-consumption. By presenting the pursuit of social status in such an extreme form, the essential nature of such a project – silly, sad and futile – is nakedly displayed.

The Hero Maker is abundantly illustrated with skilfully, wittily rendered collages created by the author/artist. Again, the source materials consist of steel engravings from the late nineteenth and early twentieth centuries, including graphics drawn from medical texts, illustrated newspapers, and other books and periodicals. Re-enforcing a central theme of the novel – mindless conformity to absurd social norms – a recurrent motif among the collages of *The Hero Maker* is that of the human head, its deformity, its replacement, injury or absence. The collages depict various objects taking the place of heads, children's heads on adult bodies, wounded heads, obliterated heads, heads separated entirely from the body and heads impaled, animal heads on human bodies, heads replaced with helmets, microcephalic heads, and heads with faces that are grotesque masks. Clearly, with heads such as these, critical thinking is out of the question.

The contemporary art world and the Hollywood film industry in their manifold absurdities are the immediate objects of ridicule in the third of Norman Rubington's collage novels, *The Boiler Maker.*[5] But, a deeper theme of the novel is the way in which language and image mediate our perception of reality, shaping our beliefs and attitudes. The "boiler maker" of the title refers not to the shot-and-a-chaser combination cherished by earnest tipplers but to an avant-garde sculptor named Luigi

Fazzoletto, also known as "Izit," founder and principal exponent of the "Mechanist Movement," whose metal constructions are indistinguishable from industrial machinery. Attracting the patronage and advocacy of the wealthy art collector Baron Hector Kleinschnitt, Izit's massive mechanical pieces initially incite

opprobrium and censure, then inspire widespread imitation, and finally achieve critical acclaim and international renown. A highly fictionalized feature film of Izit's life is undertaken by a major Hollywood studio and while the film proves to be popular and financeally successful, it causes both the Baron and Izit to be attacked by a rabble of irate sculptors who destroy the Baron's mansion and art collection, while Izit – viewed by his colleagues as having sold out to commercialism – is left destitute and forever unwell-come in the art world.

The Boiler Maker is a witty critique of the modern art world's susceptibility to gimmickry and jargon, its faddishness, fractiousness and fickleness. The book also casts a mordant eye on the schlock-blockbuster syndrome afflicting the film industry, the tasteless readiness of film writers and directors to misrepresent actual lives and events through melodrama and lurid spectacles. A common denominator between the two media – art and film – is to be found in what is viewed as a shared betrayal of their vital potential as vehicles of vision, being given over instead to devising false and shallow versions of what is real and of worth in the world. Images that could serve to elevate or liberate minds and spirits, serve instead to deceive.

In such deception language is seen to be a cunning accomplice. *The Boiler Maker* demonstrates how words impose specific interpretations upon objects and events, distorting and disguising, manipulating and misleading. "Mechanism," for instance, as a theory of art confers upon what are manifestly mere machines the status of sculptures. Considered as works of art, the machines are then much admired by art critics for their "absence of artifice," while the sculptor is lauded for the "profound dialectic in his modulation of the interior voice." Similarly, the titles assigned to individual Mechanist works, such as "Sex Drive," "Hot Bitch" and "Function of the Orgasm" cause them to be reviled by the guardians of decency and shunned by the public, though without their suggestive titles the "sculptures" would be seen as merely insipid and trivial. A further example of words defining reality occurs when the writers concocting a sensationalistic screenplay for the proposed film of Izit's life, feel compelled first to find a suitable title for the film. They decide upon "The Largest Plush in the World," a nonsensical, if titillating, phrase which bears no relation to the actual plot of the film, while their screenplay, inspired by the title, bears no relation whatever to Izit's actual life. Whatever worthy roles language and the arts might once have served in the world, expressing spiritual or philosophical truths, communicating complex feelings and states of mind, exploring perception or creating beauty, in the world of *The Boiler Maker* those noble potentials are shown to have been suffocated under an avalanche – both verbal and visual – of sham, cant and imposture.

The theme of the deployment language as an instrument to seek influence or authority over reality is also prominent in *Is That You Simon?* (1961.)[6] When Simon De Joy, a watch and clock manufacturer, launches himself into outer space aboard a homemade rocket (misnamed *Zen*) the varied interpretations of the event by the world's newspapers and citizens serve to illustrate the ways in which unaccustomed phenomena are appropriated and incorporated into pre-existing ideational patterns and ideological attitudes. In Italy, for example, *L'Osservatore* newspaper views *Zen* "not as a rocket but as a warning," while *L'Unitá* comments "*Zen* will pass just as capitalism will pass." Preoccupied with their own affairs, French newspapers consign the event to their back pages. Similarly, blasé New Yorkers ignore the occasion altogether, while "along the Mississippi, it was hailed as a symbol of the strength of the Union." Sophisticated San Franciscans can't be bothered to view the passage of the rocket through the night sky, preferring to watch it on television. Predictably, comment from the government of the U.S.S.R. interprets the occurrence in terms of Marxism. Ultimately, a cigar manufacturer in the U.S. purchases exclusive rights to De Joy's outer space communications, exploiting a remarkable historic event for commercial purposes.

Even as language can be used as a tool in an attempt to impose predetermined conceptual structures upon reality, so also in the novel do we see science and technology seeking to shape the circumstances and conditions of the material world. The watches and clocks manufactured by De Joy's plant, for instance, can be seen as part of an ongoing scientific endeavour to impose arbitrary, artificial measurement upon the fluid and elusive phenomenon of time. In a similar self-confident spirit, a host of scientists and engineers, IBM computers, the Closewitz Laboratory, the Army and the Navy and the Department of Outer Space, all strive repeatedly and in vain to effect the launch of an unmanned rocket into outer space. Significantly, when De Joy accomplishes such a launch and even succeeds in landing a spacecraft on the moon, his triumph is attributable – not to scientific rigor or technological expertise – but rather to a series of mistakes, mishaps and inadvertencies. In this way, the novel suggests the limits of human will and abilities in fashioning outcomes. Ultimately, chance trumps causality. And when it is confirmed by De Joy that already in the 12th century B.C. an expedition to the moon was achieved by Ramesses II – a theory long dismissed in scientific circles – modern science and technology suffer a decided and definitive discomfiture.

Running through *Is That You Simon?* there is a murky undercurrent of conflict and aggression, expressed in every human sphere from the political to the personal. Underlying the events of the story is the rancorous Cold War rivalry between the U.S.A. and the U.S.S.R. Additionally, there is the petulant competition between branches of the American armed services, jealous strife among members of the scientific community, and vindictive personal betrayals. Evidence of human aggression and self-assertion becomes more explicit in *Moonglow* (1969) a tale which begins with one atomic war and ends with another, while in the interim between the two conflicts malice and hostility flourish at every level.[7] *Moonglow* is the tale of Harry Moonglow, a child conceived at the very instant of the outbreak of World War III. As a consequence of having been exposed to high levels of radiation during gestation, Harry is a singular genetic mutation, one whose physical attributes are constantly in flux, as he involuntarily assumes the facial features and body shapes of a diverse array of human types. Bullied during his boyhood by other children and driven from home by his own parents, in bitterness Harry becomes a thief, before being recruited by the C.I.A. as a spy, an occupation for which he proves to be admirably suited.

The immediate post-apocalyptic era depicted in *Moonglow* is one in which human aggression persists undiscouraged and undeterred by the calamitous events that have just taken place. Survivors of the war take advantage of the chaos attendant upon mass devastation in order to pursue with impunity personal vendettas. The governments of the world quickly resume their antagonisms and "the Golden Age of the Spy" arises. Ultimately, however, due to having been made redundant by a super computer, the spies turn on their former masters, on society at large and finally on each other, committing random acts of terror, turning the cities into battlefields. In the midst of the murder and mayhem, someone contrives to unleash nuclear strikes and the world is once more reduced to rubble and radioactive ruins.

In addition to its grimly comic critique of inveterate, obdurate, perverse human destructiveness, *Moonglow* also addresses issues of technology and language. The novel makes clear the folly of developing technologies such as artificial intelligence and nuclear weapons that ultimately serve only to diminish and destroy humankind, as if our aggressive and self-aggrandizing impulses were a kind of death wish in disguise. Significantly, the story itself is related by "OSP ex-military computer (Orthophonic Syntax Pullulator.)" Apparently, in the aftermath of the second atomic war, computers have largely replaced human beings. As in *The Boiler Maker* and *Is That You Simon?* the failure of language to communicate effectively or truthfully is again a theme in *Moonglow.* We see, for example, how a dire threat uttered by a French policeman is wildly mistranslated, transforming a menacing declaration into an innocuous (if incongruous) question. We witness, too, how at one point Harry is censured by his superiors when the word "brides" is misconstrued as "bribes." Indeed, throughout the novel the words spoken by figures in the story are frequently without any relation to the situations in which they find themselves. (An innovation added to Rubington's collage illustrations in *Moonglow* is the use of speech or word balloons.) To cite but one such instance, when Harry is being arrested

for loitering in the Place St. Michel, he inquires of the arresting officer: "I can have all the cars I ever wanted?" The world of *Moonglow* is one of false appearances, pseudonyms, impersonations, replicas, non sequiturs and subterfuges, a world in which in every word and at every turn there would seem to be plentiful traps for the unwary.

The theme of cataclysm is also central to the sixth and last of Akbar del Piombo's collage novels, *Age of Ages: A Gothic Science Fiction Trip to the Apocalypse*, wherein the human situation slips by hideous increments into an abyss of chaos, madness, violence and destruction.[8] Taking as its point of departure the dystopian world depicted in George Orwell's *1984*, *Age of Ages* opens as the repressive reign of Big Brother comes to an end with his death and is succeeded and superceded by the tyrant's malign younger sibling, Little Sister. With the aim of attaining absolute control over the minds of her subjects, the new ruler effects an unholy alliance between the most advanced surveillance technology, neurotechnology and the forces of the occult, enlisting in furtherance of her project a motley body of scientists and technical experts, witches, spirit mediums, sorcerers and soothsayers.

And if such intrusive oppression were not itself sufficient tribulation for humankind, signs of "a drastically altering world" begin to manifest themselves. Suddenly, evidence of reverse evolution becomes apparent in the animal kingdom, certain of the dead return to life, and an ominous double moon appears in the night sky, whereafter madness and murder ensue and society is swept with desperate fads and cults, suicides and extremes of sensual indulgence. Al Capone is officially declared to have been a national hero and a museum is dedicated to his achievements, the Golden Calf reappears as an object of veneration and the Whore of Babylon makes her portentous entrance. Meanwhile, oblivious to consequences, scientists continue to contribute to the general decline in social order and morals by creating a myriad of monstrous new life forms, discovering new euphoria-inducing substances, and engineering life-like bio-mechanical sex-robots designed to cater to every sexual taste and preference. Even the illustrious Sir Edwin Fuzz – urgently solicited by the authorities to assist in official investigations into the grim and ever deteriorating world situation – is at loss to find an explanation or to suggest a remedy. Thus unchecked by any human restraint or resource, the apocalypse advances inexorably toward havoc, collapse and utter devastation.

Might it be the case that in this instance Sir Edwin Fuzz is unable to discover a perpetrator to the crime under investigation because the solution lies beyond the purview of criminal science and resides, instead, in the realm of the metaphysical? Is the apocalypse in some unknown way a response to human folly and depravity? Or is the extraordinary wave of debauched and destructive human behaviour that engulfs the world a consequence of the apocalypse? Or is there an implication here that order in the natural world is not immutable but at best tenuous and temporary? Certainly, the sudden erratic nature of the physical world (reverse evolution, the double moon, resurrections, etc.) may be seen to be mirrored in the outbreak of lawless human behaviour. The civilized world is suddenly assailed to an unparalleled degree by uncontrolled compulsions given untrammelled expression: the pursuit of power (Little Sister and her minions,) of plunder (criminal gangs and sundry muggers,) and pleasure (the erotically obsessed sensualists with their sex-robots.)

The collages in *Age of Ages* portray a world in which conventional reality is no longer stable but ever shifting. Dissimilar phenomena and even temporal periods collide, the incredible invades the ordinary: ancient gods drive modern racing cars, fish swim placidly through the air, extinct animals invade homes and buildings, roman gladiators mug passersby on the streets of New York city, smiling nudes recline before an onrushing locomotive, spear-carrying armour-clad warriors stand guard at the Pentagon, an orbiting open air space colony passes above a giant antique Victrola, sanitation workers exorcise demons from a victim of possession, an automated trashcan deflowers a young woman. Certitude, order and pattern are overthrown and the world stands revealed as tentative, equivocal, a farcical flux, a comic nightmare, an unsolved riddle.

At one dramatic moment in *Age of Ages,* Sir Edwin Fuzz wonders aloud: "Has the battle for men's minds been won? And if so, by whom?" The question might be said to resonate back through all the Akbar del Piombo collage novels an underlying theme of which is human folly in its myriad forms. Religion, philosophy and ideals of personal conscience and social justice all alike bid us to seek the good and the true, but, as history and biography can attest, all too often our best intentions are undermined or overwhelmed by forces from without and from within, forces that seek, instead, to diminish our integrity, our individual autonomy and personal agency and, in effect, seize control of our minds. Such forces are the targets of satirical critique in the del Piombo collage novels: unquestioned conventions and received opinions, human vanity and aggression, status seeking, conformity, hedonism and avarice, narrow moralism, and a gullible trust in authority, technology, language and consensus reality.

A number of motifs in the collage novels can be seen to reflect the radical instability and accelerating change of the era through which the author and artist Norman Rubington lived: the Great Depression, the rise of fascism, World War II, the Korean War and the Cold War, postwar affluence and the advent of television, computers and automation, mass communications, mass marketing and mass consumption, the growth of large bureaucracies and large corporations, the space program, atomic weapons and the threat of nuclear annihilation. To alert and reflective minds of Rubington's generation the world must have seemed erratic, precarious and unpredictable in the extreme, a world in which the individual was under siege from multiple systems. Hence, I think, the distrust of science and authority, of fads and mass movements and of linguistic and cultural codes that may be seen to pervade the Akbar del Piombo collage novels. Similar anxieties are to be found in the works of fellow satirists of Rubington's generation, including Terry Southern, William S. Burroughs, Joseph Heller, Kurt Vonnegut Jr. and Lenny Bruce.

Even among fellow satirists and hip humourists of his generation, Norman Rubington's collage novels are notable for their unique combination of the verbal and the visual, as well as for the distinctive wit and wild sense of the absurd that inform them. (E.g. *Age of Ages* in which "mutiny aboard a one-man submarine" occurs.) It is discouraging to discover that at present all of the Akbar del Piombo collage novels are out-of-print. This is regrettable since they are very far from being dated artifacts of the postwar hip sensibility but are, instead, perennially pertinent satires, imbued with an unruly and hallucinatory humour. It is to be hoped that soon some enterprising small press will rescue them from the undeserved oblivion into which they seem now to have fallen.

NOTES

[1] Written by Norman Rubington under the name of Akbar del Piombo: *Who Pushed Paula?* (1956), *Skirts* (1956), *Cosimo's Wife* (1957), *The Traveller's Companion* (1957) and *The Fetish Crowd* (1959.) All published by the Olympia Press, Paris. There is a brief account of Rubington's early years in Paris in *Left Bank, Right Bank* by Joseph Barry, London: 1952, pp. 71-72. Barry writes of Rubington as being "perhaps the most talented of the younger American artists in Paris" p. 71.

[2] With regard to viewing Rubington's collage novels as speculative fiction, the only review of the Akbar del Piombo books that I have been able to locate appeared in *The Magazine of Fantasy & Science Fiction,* vol. 24, no. 2, February 1963: "Books: *Fuzz Against Junk, Is that you Simon?, The Boiler Maker, The Hero Maker,*" by Avram Davidon, pp. 33-34.

[3] *Fuzz Against Junk* by Akbar del Piombo, Paris: Olympia Press, 1959; New York: Citadel Press, 1961; London: New English Library, 1966; New York: Beach Books, 1969; *Rolling Stone* nos. 33, 34, 35, 36, 1969. A French translation titled *L'Anticame* was published in Paris by La Grande Séverine in 1960. The American slang term "fuzz" used to designate the police was widely used among criminals, hobos and carnival workers for several decades before gaining currency among the hipsters and Beats of the 1950s. See *Flappers 2 Rappers: American Youth Slang* by Tom Dalzell published Merriam-Webster, Springfield, Mass. 1996, pp. 91,140.

[4] *The Hero Maker* by Akbar del Piombo, Paris: The Olympia Press, 1960. Reprinted bound with *Fuzz Against Junk*, London: New English Library, 1966.

[5] *The Boiler Maker* by Akbar del Piombo, published simultaneously in Paris by The Olympia Press and in New York by The Citadel Press, 1961.

[6] *Is That You Simon?* by Akbar del Piombo, published simultaneously in Paris by The Olympia Press and in New York by The Citadel Press, 1961.

[7] *Moonglow* by Akbar del Piombo, New York: Beach Books, 1969.

[8] *Age of Ages: A Gothic Science Fiction Trip to the Apocalypse* appeared in serial form in *Heavy Metal* April 1977, pp. 79-82; May 1977, pp. 66-68; June 1977, pp. 69-71; August 1977, pp. 53-56; and February 1978, pp. 69-72.

"CURIOUS AND NOT UN-POETICAL IMAGININGS"

A Forgotten Specimen of Victorian Cannabis Writing

"Imagination is the dream of the Unconscious."
Benjamin DeCasseres

During the 19th century, even as explorers journeyed to the last dark recesses and remote wastes of the world, and as archaeologists excavated fabled kingdoms and uncovered lost epochs of human history, expeditions and excavations of another order entirely were being undertaken by individuals situated in rooms in Paris, London and New York City. With the aid of opium, nitrous oxide and hashish, daring excursions were made by them into the farther reaches of the mind and "digs" conducted down into the deeper strata of consciousness. The better known accounts of these ventures include Thomas De Quincey's *Confessions of an English Opium Eater* (1821), Fitz Hugh Ludlow's

The Hasheesh Eater (1857), and Charles Baudelaire's *Les Paradis Artificiels* (1860). Less known, though equally of interest in this regard, are the writings of Humphry Davy and Benjamin Blood on nitrous oxide, and those of Théophile Gautier and Jacques-Joseph Moreau on hashish. Yet, altogether lost to sight, it would seem, is an anonymously written booklet published in London in 1884, titled *Confessions of an English Hachish Eater.* Although the little volume did not go entirely unnoticed at the time of its publication, this curious account of solitary inward voyages to mysterious regions of the mind and exploratory soundings of deeper layers of the self slipped quickly into oblivion. The booklet has never been reprinted, nor has it ever been excerpted or cited in any of the various anthologies of cannabis or drug writings. Copies (even in library collections) are exceedingly rare.

Confessions of an English Hachish Eater is a paperbound booklet of 114 pages. The publisher was George Redway and the booklet was issued as part of "Redway's Shilling Series." Other titles by the same publisher include *The Handbook of Palmistry, Chirognomancy, The Anatomy of Tobacco, Theosophy, Religion and Occult Science, Phallicism,* and *Bibliotheca Arcana seu Catalogus Librorum Penetralium* (this last a work of which I shall have something to say at a later point.) As a publisher, George Redway seems to have been inclined toward esoterica, occultism and topics outside of the mainstream of Victorian taste. The text of *Confessions* (the title clearly an homage to De Quincey's classic personal narrative) consists of five sections, each titled and assigned a Roman numeral. The first two sections deal in the main with the history, nature, preparation and proper consumption of hashish, together with brief accounts of certain of the author's experiences of hashish intoxication. Sections three to five are made up of "dream-stories," that is to say extended narratives of the author's hashish reveries, followed by some concluding remarks on the part of the author.

Already from the opening sentences and early paragraphs of *Confessions*, it is evident that the anonymous author is well-read with regard to his topic. He acknowledges the inspiration he derived from reading descriptions by (European) hashish pioneers Alexandre Dumas, Théophile Gautier and Bayard Taylor, and makes allusions to *Materia Medica*, to *The British Pharmacopaeia*, and to scientific research on hashish carried out by medical doctors Alexander Christison and William Brooke O'Shaugnessy. With sober earnestness and barely restrained zeal, the author describes the manner in which he prepares his own hashish, using freshly imported cannabis from Persia and India, selecting only the flowering tops of the plants, and then macerating, pressing, distilling and evaporating the substance until he has produced a viscous, resinous extract which in carefully measured doses he then consumes orally.

The psychoactive effects of hashish thus administered can be dramatic, comparable to those of a psychedelic drug. The author recounts how during his first experience of hashish intoxication his mind seemed to quit his body and travel to remote locations: "It visited the strand of a calm and moonlit sea, in whose waters beautiful women bathed, laughing. Thence it was transported to the sward of a forest glade full of the music of birds that flitted hither and thither. Again, with equal suddenness, it was carried upwards through the crisp air of night to a mountain peak, whence all around was visible in the starlight; and I felt myself alone in a world of ice-fields and avalanches." He finds that hashish seems to enhance his musical abilities, his sense of the ridiculous, and his appetite, and he is relieved to discover that (unlike alcohol) the drug has no unpleasant after-effects. In brief, he pronounces: "I have no ill word to speak of it."

The author is, however, not unconscious of the drug's darker potentials, admitting that at times under the influence of hashish the sense of profound calm and "sublime spiritual elevation" he enjoys can be slowly undermined by insidious unease or suddenly interrupted by sensations of hideous horror. Indeed, a common denominator among a number of the hashish reveries he recounts is that of enchantment gradually giving way to gloom or alarm. In one such reverie, the author follows "a divinely lovely sylph" down into a dark cavern where she turns into a baleful bat-like creature. In another hashish-induced trance, he partakes in imagination of passionate, ecstatic love with a woman, only to witness their romance end in madness and murder.

In parts three, four and five of *Confessions*, the author presents three examples of what he terms "dream stories," that is detailed, dramatized narratives inspired by his hashish reveries. These tales, according to his account, are edited versions of what was at the time experienced by him as a succession of images, "all haze and mystery." Two of the dream stories – "Vox Clamantis" and "Gnothi Seauton" – are melodramatic allegories, both treating themes of deception and self-deception. In both stories, male figures fall into error due to selfishness and a self-indulgence. In the former story, the young protagonist is ultimately undeceived and redeemed, while in the latter tale the faithless, rapacious antagonist ends by being forever confined in the company of an embodiment of his own "foul, hideous self."

As literary fiction neither story can be said to possess particular distinction, but both contain intriguing elements of oneiric strangeness: imagery of mists and spectres, portentous lightning-blasted tree trunks, ominous clouds and a sinister glittering snake, a hidden paradisiacal realm, a remote cave filled with bright jewels, and sensuous descriptions of hues, fragrances, sounds and tastes and all that is luxurious, delicious and exquisite. Of greater interest and originality, though, is the story titled "A Strange Journey," which recounts the author's imaginary experiences during an evening excursion through London streets while under the influence of hashish. This tale would seem to have been subjected to less secondary revision by the author than the previous two texts and strikes the reader as likely to have been based on an actual experience on the part of the author.

"A Strange Journey" might be compared to a technicolor, animated film, something like a collaboration between Tex Avery and Salvador Dali. The story begins solidly and specifically anchored in the author's visit to a surgeon friend at Hammersmith, with mundane details of their dinner and conversation. In the course of his visit, the author swallows a portion of hashish, and only as he departs the doorstep of his host does he begin to feel the effects of the drug. At this point, the narrative becomes surreal. The author becomes aware that he has been "liberated from the ordinary shackles of the body," discovering that he possesses the ability to take flight through the air, a mode of locomotion he finds to be both agreeable and efficient. At length, he discovers that he is being pursued in his aerial travels by a thousand tiny, jolly sprites, whose antics and hilarity the author finds irresistibly amusing. He joins them in their merriment and after a time finds himself alone with one of their company whose rosy, gleeful face is crowned by "a large red, curiously forked, carrot-like proboscis, which it moved at will, just as the octopus moves its tentacles." The author soon perceives that he has mounted to a great height in the air and can see far below him an immense, empty ocean.

At this moment, his outlandish companion begins to metamorphose, miraculously growing legs of a prodigious length that reach down into the depths of the ocean below. Simultaneously, the creature's remarkable nose undergoes extensive modifications: "the carrot-like proboscis was growing at a wonderful rate, and shooting out new tentacles with great speed and at very frequent intervals. These tentacles were of a bright orange colour, and, in shape, much like attenuated spoons, the bowls being, however, flattened and covered on both sides with round white spots." Embraced and enclosed by these vivid nasal tentacles, the author finds his way to the creature's mouth into which he enters, descending thence into the throat. His presence there causes a convulsive reaction on the part of his host and he is violently expelled. He now finds himself in pieces, his head, arms and legs pursuing each other through the air, attempting in vain to reassemble themselves. When, at last, the fragments assume their accustomed places, the author discovers that his body is now made of wax and that he is lying on a bed of cotton-wool. He fears that in this delicate condition he may break, dent or melt, then realizes that his soft bed is not composed of cotton-wool but of gun-cotton (a highly flammable, explosive agent). Fire-flies ignite the gun-cotton and the author sees himself disappear "in a cloud of ill-smelling smoke."

The author maintains that through all of these extraordinary events, he felt no alarm but only curiosity, amusement and a kind of philosophical resignation. Even after having experienced the total dissolution of his physical body in the explosion described above, his consciousness, he relates, continues to exist in a disembodied form in which he feels himself to be "in a state of complete and absolute bliss that did not permit me to feel my loss." Ultimately, as the influence of the drug diminishes and normal awareness returns to him, and the author discovers that he has somehow returned to his own residence, has undressed, and gone to bed, having performed all the customary night time tasks in the usual manner.

Despite their occasional disconcerting turns, the author heartily relishes and cherishes his hashish adventures, declaring that he has found the drug to be "a nepenthes, a sweet bringer of delicious oblivion, and a generous parent of delightful dreams." He can see no evidence that his judicious, intermittent indulgence in the drug has to any degree damaged him either physically or mentally. Dismissing cautions against the consumption of hashish as mere self-righteous moralizing of the kind characteristic of prigs, prudes and puritans, the author defiantly declares that he hopes "to enjoy its effects many times again."

Perhaps due to its rarity and obscurity, *Confessions of an English Hachish Eater* has been neglected by scholars of drug literature. While not a lost classic of the genre, this unusual booklet is noteworthy as an early account of recreational cannabis consumption in Victorian England, and represents a lone link between the experimental, inspirational use of drugs by the Romantics in the early 19th century and that of the Decadents in the *fin-de- siècle* era. In the spirit of both these cultural counter currents, the anonymous author of *Confessions* takes a stand on the side of the insurgent imagination as against the prevailing rationalist, materialist ethos of the age.

The critical reception of *Confessions* was muted and mixed. The *Daily Chronicle* pronounced it "a weird little book," the *Whitehall Review* found "a sort of bizarre attraction" in it, while the *Lincolnshire Chronicle* thought it "charmingly written," and worthy of comparison to De Quincey's celebrated *Confessions of an English Opium Eater.* Other reviewers worried that the book might encourage indulgence in hashish. "Weak minds may generate a morbid curiosity if stimulated in this direction," warned the *Bradford Observer,* a view in which the *Edinburgh Courant* concurred, writing "we would not be surprised if some foolish individuals did endeavour to procure some of the drug, with a view to experience the sensation described by the author of this clever *brochure.*"

And who, indeed, might have been the author of "this clever *brochure?*" Considerable evidence points to the authorship of William Laird Clowes (1856-1905). The argument for considering Clowes as the anonymous writer of *Confessions of an English Hachish Eater* derives from an article titled "An Amateur Assassin" appearing under Clowes' name in *Belgravia* magazine, vol. 31, issue 123, 1877, or about seven years before the publication of the anonymous *Confesssions.* The article recounts Clowes' personal experiences in consuming homemade hashish, employing many of the same phrases and formulations later to appear in *Confessions.* Apart from these correspondences, "An Amateur Assassin" also makes reference to a number of the same experiences and incidents as *Confessions,* and puts forward many of the same observations and comments as expressed in the latter work. Comparing the two texts, it is clear that the author of both is the selfsame person.

As mentioned at a prior point in this writing, George Redway of London was also the publisher of a book titled *Bibliotheca Arcana seu Catalogus Liborum Penetralium* (1885), "being brief notices of books that have been secretly printed, prohibited by law, seized, anathematised, burnt or Bowdlerised."

On the title page of the book, the author is given as "Speculator Morum," an obvious nom-de-plume intended to avert disrepute falling upon the author of the volume, which consists of an inventory of an extensive subterranean erotic literature held in "the secret cabinets of our public or private museums or libraries." In fact, the compilers of this indecorous volume were two venturesome scholars, one of whom is William Laird Clowes and the other the Reverend (!) John McLellan, who also wrote the preface to the book. In common with *Confessions of an English Hachish Eater,* this subversive endeavor suggests a penchant on the part of Clowes to dissent from certain of the prevailing attitudes of his age, in this instance sexual prudery.

In *Confessions of an English Hachish Eater,* the author does not suggest that the strange tales with which he has returned from his hashish adventures possess notable literary merit. He modestly (and accurately, I think) characterizes his dream-stories as "curious and not un-poetical imaginings," and compares them to "lightning flashes upon the scenery of a dark and unknown landscape." That dark landscape is one normally accessible only in dreams, a mysterious internal world with its own geography and geology, where the psychological structures and culturally conditioned habits of mind that regulate and sustain our everyday lives are no longer operative.

The author notes how in these remote regions and deeper substrata of the mind, a blurring or merging of identities and contraries takes place. In one of his accounts of a hashish reverie he remarks how two separate scenes, two distinct conditions somehow converge and coalesce: "The one merged into the other, I scarcely know how. They were separated and yet intimately blending, just like dissolving views." Similarly, elsewhere, the author comments on the phenomenon of shifting, merging identities that takes place in his reveries, remarking upon the way in which in one such reverie the figure of a young man "was sometimes myself and sometimes another," and noting how in the same reverie four other figures "were different, but yet strangely and exactly alike." The ambiguity of personal identity is reflected in at least one instance where a passage narrated in the third person suddenly becomes one told in the first person.

The author also discerns that the mind is multi-levelled and that below the threshold of conscious awareness there are selves within the self and an autonomous poetic faculty, a hidden river of images, chronicles and conceptions. Implicitly, *Confessions of an English Hachish Eater* affirms the mystery of the human mind and argues for a broadening of consciousness to include those modes of being and awareness that are to be found outside the jurisdiction of the primary personality and the rational brain. These perspectives which would seem to have been regarded as utterly peripheral in the 19th century may now be seen to have been prophetic.

A FEW FAR-FLUNG FRAGMENTS OF FORGOTTEN KEROUACIANA

There are still a few odd jottings and stray scribbles from the pen of Jack Kerouac – elusive bits and bobs published during the author's lifetime – that remain unrecorded in bibliographies and/or uncollected in compilations of his writings. Admittedly, these fugitive fragments of Kerouac's writing are not necessarily all lost literary gems, but I would argue that they merit the attention of readers seriously interested in Kerouac's life and work.

The following account of scattered scraps of Kerouac's writing is by no means definitive or comprehensive. I have not included juvenilia, early sports reporting for *The Lowell Sun* or posthumous publications, but limited my choice of texts to biographical and literary items and letters actually submitted by the author to various publications in which they were subsequently printed. What follows below is intended as a survey of certain far-strewn, neglected bits of Kerouaciana that I have discovered or been made aware of. And let me take the opportunity here to acknowledge the valuable help extended to me in this endeavour by the eminent Beat Generation scholar, Dave Moore.

One largely overseen category of stray compositions by Kerouac consists of the short contributor's notes written by the author for the sundry periodicals and anthologies in which his work appeared. Kerouac's biographical notes – each individually formulated by him for the particular publication printing his work – are unique compositions and interesting for their presentation of his life, his literary influences, as well as his attitudes and aims as seen by him at the time of writing. The autobiographical statement that accompanies the publication of "The Origins of Joy in Poetry" and two poems in *Chicago Review*, Spring 1958, is, perhaps, the most curious of all of the author's autobiographical notes. The note outlines the usual information, date and place of birth, education, sports, early writings, experiences in the merchant marine, travels, but concludes with a disconcerting pronouncement: "... so now I can only say my motto is I DON'T KNOW I DON'T CARE AND IT DOESN'T MAKE ANY DIFFERENCE (my final philosophical statement)." [1]

For those familiar with Kerouac's writing up to and after this point, this bald assertion seems uncharacteristically despairing, even nihilistic.

By way of contrast, in an autobiographical statement appearing in *Big Table*, No. 1, Spring 1959, Kerouac again lists his various occupations (railroad brakeman, seaman, etc.) but represents himself as a "student" of eight writers and two spiritual traditions. (The latter seeming to contradict the despondence and weary, fatalistic indifference implied in the *Chicago Review* note cited above.) The writers from whom he

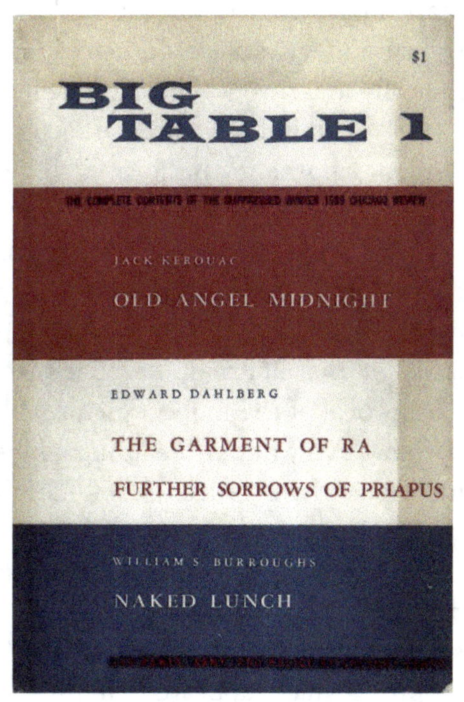

credits inspiration and instruction are William Blake, Arthur Rimbaud, Herman Melville, Mark Twain, Walt Whitman, Emily Dickinson and James Joyce. This list differs significantly from the personal pantheon Kerouac enumerates one year later in his biographical note in *The New American Poetry*: Jack London, Ernest Hemingway, William Saroyan, Fyodor Dostoevsky and Johann Wolfgang von Goethe. [2]]The spiritual traditions of which he states he is a student in the same *Big Table* note he names as being "the Tao and the Mahayana Aryan Buddhism of Gotama." [3] Again, this is noteworthy, not only in opposition to the *Chicago Review* statement, but also since only a year later in the "Author's Introduction" to *Lonesome Traveller*, Kerouac describes himself as a "strange solitary crazy Catholic mystic." [4] Clearly, these were years in which the author underwent transformative psychological and spiritual experiences (see *Big Sur*) that altered him radically in terms of the beliefs he held.

A handful of unremarked, uncollected publications by Kerouac appear in the form of letters written to the editors of various magazines. The author's aim in two of these letters is to correct what he sees as misapprehensions concerning the nature of the Beat Generation. A letter to the editor of *Escapade* magazine, titled "A Communication," appears in the April, 1960 issue of that journal. Kerouac's short message expresses his disapproval of the motion picture, "The Beat Generation," which he views as a work of "insulting ugliness" for its preposterous and malicious characterization of harmless, bookish bohemians as psychotic criminals. [5]

Similarly, a letter to the editor of *Playboy* magazine, printed in the March 1961 issue, is a response by Kerouac to a story written by Roger Price titled "Father Brother and the Cool Colony," which appeared in the December 1960 issue of the

magazine. To Kerouac, Price's story was a further example of the phenomenon later named "beatsploitation," that is the ignorant, commercial caricaturing of Beat figures – a practice not uncommon in film, television and printed media during the time. In his letter, Kerouac states emphatically that no such entity as a "cool colony" exists, nor should it exist. The notion, he writes, is as ludicrous as that of a "square colony." Kerouac deplores both Price's attribution to the Beats of a sneering contempt for squares, and Price's depiction of Beats as expressing superior scorn for certain occupations or professions. Such distinctions, Kerouac insists, were not made among the original Beats. What was, instead, seen by them as being of consequence in any individual was "the spirituality of the person." [6]

Both of these letters show Kerouac attempting to exercise some kind of restraining or directing influence over the concept of which he was the originator but over which he felt he was losing control to poseurs and opportunists.

In a similar manner, Kerouac is quoted by *New York Journal-American* columnist, Louis Sobol, as having written a letter or otherwise stated that he takes exception to being classified as a "beatnik," and to being compared to Norman Mailer in terms of political views and ambitions. Kerouac is cited by Sobol as saying: "I am seriously devoted to my writing, and want to be considered a serious writer. I am a peace-loving citizen with nothing but love for my fellow men. I have no particular political leanings. It is not my fault that certain so-called Bohemian elements have found in my writings something to hang their peculiar Beatnik theories on. To repeat, I am a writer – author of some books that have found favour with readers – but I hope before I die, I'll be recognized for what I really am – someone who never was and never cared to be of the Beatnik clan." [7]

On the basis of the letters described above, we may infer that Kerouac saw the integrity of his original vision of the Beat Generation as being threatened on two fronts. From one direction came the menace of facile, crass, commercial misappropriation of the Beat idea, while from another direction came the peril of aberrant encroachments upon the Beat spirit by self-identified followers. In this regard, another, as yet uncollected bit of writing from the author's pen addresses in as definitive a manner as possible the topic of the Beat Generation. It is, in fact, a definition of the movement solicited from Kerouac by the editor of the *American College Dictionary*. As concisely and precisely as possible, Kerouac writes: "Beat Generation: Members of the generation that came of age after World War II, who espouse mystical detachment and relaxation of social and sexual tensions, supposedly as a result of disillusionment stemming from the cold war." [8] This definition attempts to preclude the kind of sneering intellectual superiority misattributed to Beats as well as the fractious leftward political turn of some Beat writers that Kerouac feared would attenuate and ultimately displace the essentially spiritual character of the Beat Generation, as he conceived it.

A further uncollected letter to the editor of *Escapade*, printed in the June 1960 issue, is a defense by the author of an earlier article written by him on bullfighting that appeared in the December 1959 number of *Escapade*. Kerouac's disapproving description of a bull fight he attended in Mexico had provoked among the magazine's readership several *aficionados* of the sport who wrote to the editor mocking and deriding what they saw

as Kerouac's sentimentality. In his written response to the reaction generated by his piece on bullfighting, Kerouac gives no ground but reaffirms his sense of the essential cruelty of taunting, torturing and killing bulls for sport, stating emphatically: "I do not believe it is a grand thing for men to prove their goddam dignity at the expense of some dumb beast." [9] Readers familiar with the author's gentle ethos will recognize here a theme recurrent in Kerouac's writing. Kerouac's rare indignation is reserved for those who knowingly inflict harm on their fellow humans and creatures with whom they share life and sentience.

On a more affirmative note, Kerouac writes to the editor of *Metronome* (No. 5, May 1961) praising the whole of the former issue of the (jazz-oriented) journal, and singling out for particular praise a piece written by Lenny Bruce. (This would have been "Lenny Bruce Cries Foul," in the March 1961 issue of *Metronome*.) This latter letter – brief though it is – seems to me more characteristic of the author who was by nature far more inclined to be generous and inclusive, to praise and embrace, than to criticize and condemn.

A relatively obscure, still uncollected piece by Kerouac, entitled "Dave," appears in the literary review, *Kulchur*, (No. 3, 1961). [10] Preceding the piece, a note by Kerouac states that it was "Dictated to me in Mexico City 1952 by David Tercerero – died November 1954." Readers of William Burroughs and Jack Kerouac will recognize the figure of Dave Tercerero (actually Tesorero). He appears under the name of "Old Ike" in Burroughs's novel, *Junkie* (1953), and is mentioned in Kerouac's *Tristessa* (1960) as "Dave," former husband of Tristessa, already dead at the time of the novel's narrative: "dead Dave my old buddy of previous years dead now" (p. 12) Tristessa keeps a photo of him on the wall of her tenement apartment. Interestingly, Dave Tercerero also appears as a player in Kerouac's fantasy baseball game, playing both for the Thunderbirds and the Cincinnati Blacks. (See *Kerouac at Bat: Fantasy Sports and the King of the Beats* by Isaac Gewirtz, New York, 2009, p. 62, p. 66.)

"Dave" is a first person account of Dave Tercerero's life from boyhood to young manhood. It is a tale of poverty, adversity, danger and struggle. The narrator recounts his misadventures from a peripheral participation in the Mexican Revolution to a career as a thief on both sides of the border, relating the circumstances of his incarcerations, escapes and

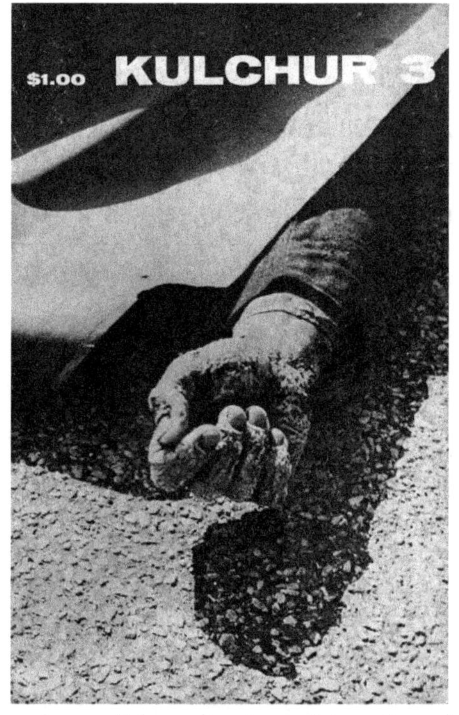

morphine addiction. Beyond the intrinsic interest of the events themselves, the text is noteworthy as an example of Kerouac's fascination and empathy with socially marginal figures. Readers will recall the author's many sympathetic depictions of hoboes, ex-cons, junkies, prostitutes, eccentrics and outsiders. "Dave" is also significant as an illustration of Kerouac's informal literary-aesthetic sensibility, his predilection for spontaneity and for an oral, candid quality in writing. Dave's account of his life may lack eloquence, formal organization and grammatical correctness, but it possesses the authority of personal truth and a broader human pertinence.

A final fragment of forgotten, uncollected Kerouaciana is to be found among the pages of an academic journal called *Twentieth Century Studies* published by the University of Kent at Canterbury. This brief appearance in print, among the very last during the author's life, consists of a 67-word reply made by Kerouac to a survey conducted by the journal among prominent authors on the topic of the sexual revolution and the depiction of sexuality in literature. A section of the magazine, under the title "The Professional Viewpoint," was set aside to present the written statements the authors had made in response to the journal's query.

Kerouac's statement is personal and poetic. He declares that for his own part the sexual revolution began when he was sixteen. He describes a scene when he attempted to kiss his girlfriend through a wire screen door. In response, his girlfriend eagerly, vigorously threw open the door and engaged with him in a passionate kiss. Kerouac concludes his anecdote with the phrase: "And we sang Sanity beneath the trees." [11]

Kerouac's anecdote celebrates the overcoming of artificial barriers (the screen door) to natural joy, and the momentary recovery of Edenic harmony. This sense of the essential innocence of sexual love is recurrent in Kerouac's writing, though often tempered by an awareness of the destructive aspects of the sexual appetite. As if to affirm that an ideal romantic-erotic encounter (such as that depicted in the anecdote) may be experienced as a kind of sacrament, rather than a lapse or transgression, Kerouac ends his contribution to the forum on the sexual revolution with a closing salutation to the reader, a blessing: God be with you.

Scrutinizing these scattered scraps of the sprawling Kerouacian chronicle, we see an author engaged in defining and defending the vision that animates his writing, a vision of the mad, melancholy, heroic and holy nature of human life. While they are not neglected masterpieces awaiting rediscovery, these uncollected minor pieces make up a varied and vivid lot that serve to extend and deepen our knowledge of Jack Kerouac's continual evolution and abiding concerns as a writer.

NOTES

[1] "Notes on Contributors," *Chicago Review*, Vol. 12, no. 1, Spring 1958, p. 108.

[2] "Biographical Note" by Jack Kerouac, *The New American Poetry 1945 – 1960*, edited by Donald M. Allen (New York: 1960) pp. 438-39.

[3] . "Notes on Contributors" by Jack Kerouac, *Big Table*, No. 1, Spring 1959, p. 2.

[4] "Author's Introduction" by Jack Kerouac, *Lonesome Traveler* (New York: 1960) vi.

[5] "Barbs and Balm," *Escapade*, Vol. IV, No. 3, April 1960, p. 66.

[6] Dear Playboy" letter from Jack Kerouac, *Playboy*, Vol. 8, No. 3, March 1961, p. 5.

[7] "Kerouac Protests Legend" by Louis Sobol, *New York Journal-American*, Thursday, December 8, 1960.

[8] *The American College Dictionary*, Clarence L. Barnhart, editor-in-chief, (New York: 1962).

[9] "Barbs and Balm", *Escapade,* Vol. V, No. 4, June 1960, p. 68.

[10] *Kulchur,* No. 3, January 1961, pp. 3-5.

[11] "The Professional Viewpoint," response by Jack Kerouac, *Twentieth Century Studies*, Vol. 1, March 1969, p. 118.

"WOUNDS OF WONDER"

Poems from the Greenberg Manuscripts
Edited, and with an essay, by James Laughlin
New, expanded edition edited by Garrett Caples
New Directions Poetry Pamphlet no. 24
New York: 2019, 72 pp. $11.95

These poems – over a hundred years old – are surpassingly strange. They are among the strangest, I believe, in the history of American letters, and the story behind them is sad and strange.

The Greenberg Manuscripts consist of circa 600 holograph pages of poems, prose and plays written by Samuel Bernard Greenberg (1893 – 1917) an impoverished, untutored young jewish immigrant from Austria – an ardent reader of classic English poetry with only a sixth grade education

– who died a lonely, untimely and tragic death at the age of 23 in the tuberculosis ward of the Manhattan State Hospital on Wards Island, New York city. After Greenberg's death, his manuscripts (written in notebooks and cheap tablets and on loose sheets of paper, including calendar leaves and wrapping paper) passed into the hands of William Murrell Fisher who had befriended the young poet, lending him books during his long illness and encouraging him in his writing. Six years after Samuel Greenberg's death, late in the year 1923, Fisher showed some of Greenberg's poems to the poet Hart Crane (1899-1932.) Crane was immediately taken with the poems, indeed, he was seized by excitement, pacing the floor and declaiming them aloud. Crane made his own copies of the poems, and ultimately appropriated from Greenberg's poetry numerous images, phrases and entire poems, incorporating them into his own work without acknowledging their source.

Only after Crane's death were the Greenberg poems discovered as having served as uncredited sources for certain of Crane's poems. This disclosure then led to an interest on the part of some scholars and poets into Greenberg's own work, previously unknown to any but Fisher and Crane. The first appearance of Samuel Greenberg's poetry in book form under his own name was a 32 page volume in stapled wrappers, edited and with an introduction by James Laughlin (founder and editor of New Directions Publishing) printed in 1939 and titled *Poems from the Greenberg Manuscripts*. This rare booklet has now – after 80 years – been reprinted by New Directions in a "new, expanded edition," edited by Garrett Caples. The incisive original introduction by Laughlin has been supplemented by an equally insightful *Preface* by Caples, and the original selection of poems has been expanded to include ten additional poems together with a letter and two prose pieces by Greenberg.

Greenberg's poetry is cast in various forms, including end-rhymed quatrains and unrhymed quatrains, blank verse sonnets and free verse. His poems not infrequently contain misspellings and erratic punctuation, as well as grammatical, syntactical and lexical errors; they mix archaisms and poeticisms with mysterious word coinages. They tend toward the effusive and rhapsodic, are marked by ellipsis and incongruity, by shifts and juxtapositions, and by rolling metrical phrases and amazing sweeps and leaps of language. They are, as Hart Crane wrote to a friend, the poems of "a Rimbaud in embryo." [1] Or, as the poet Philip Lamantia observed of them, Greenberg's poems are "veritable *wounds of wonder.*" [2]

Recurrent among Samuel Greenberg's poems are images of light and color. The things of the world are seen by him to glimmer and shine, they glow, are luminous, splendorous, brilliant or bright; they are of cerulean, rose, ruby, silver, violet, gold, pink, green, yellow. The beauty of the world, its light and its hues, can seem to reflect a truer Beauty beyond the visible world. Yet "the sordid earth" is also known to the poet as a realm of "solemn woes," of foulness and staleness, fear and pain, where mortals rave under "vanishing skies," and where "Love is truly a lost jewel." Also recurrent in Greenberg's poems are allusions to divinity and the sacred: to Jehovah, to God and the Lord, to deity and saints, to prayer and the soul, to psalms and "spiritual thought," to the heavens and eternity, and to "the spiritual gate" we seek to discover, beyond which lies the redemption and restitution of all things. At times the poet laments his particular plight, his doomed life: "a stricken creature I am," "an extricable prisoner bound /to essence" from which he strives to emancipate himself, but Greenberg senses that the poetry he creates participates somehow in a larger mystery: "that which rises from my inner tomb / Is but the haste of the starry splendor dome." The exalted lyricism of Greenberg's poetry strains against the limits of language striving to express a visionary experience akin to that of poets such as George Herbert, Thomas Traherne, William Blake and Gerard Manley Hopkins.

Certain of Greenberg's poems seem almost to be transcriptions of dreams, charged with the strange, swift drama of dreams. "Conduct," one of the group of poems enigmatically titled "Sonnets of Apology," possesses a vivid, oneiric quality:

> By a peninsula, the painter sat and
> Sketched the uneven valley groves
> The apostle gave alms to the
> Meek, the volcano burst
> In fusive sulphur and hurled
> Rocks and ore into the air,
> Heaven's sudden change at
> The drawing tempestuous
> Darkening shade of Dense clouded Hues
> The wanderer soon chose
> His spot of rest, they bore the
> Chosen hero upon their shoulders
> Whom they greatly admired, as,
> The Beach tide summer of people desired.

Other poems by Greenberg , such as "The Pale Impromtu" and "Tusks of Blood" seem to be transcriptions of a discourse below conscious awareness, disjunct, fecund, a welter, a torrent, a tumult of words:

> Hidden winds perspired foul – as
> a palmed rose
> The well shade
> Urgent fears
> Eyes jealousy
> painted mirth
> royal flesh
> candle salve
> consumed moon
> And here, the ash tray was Blown!

(from "The Pale Impromptu")

> The brief gong of Greek gales
> Have found the inner teeth alone
> Here, listen someone is calling
> …
> thy Mongolian fringe of foul perfume
> The falling off—weep for a keep
> That O shade salons its pierce

(from "Tusks of Blood")

Also included in this edition of *Poems from the Greenberg Manuscripts* is a long, lyrical letter titled "Between Historical Life," written by the poet to his brother Daniel, together with two surreal, stream-of-consciousness prose pieces: "Poetical Development" and "Yiddish, or Impressions in Sentiment." The letter, written by Greenberg from his hospital bed in 1916, the year before his death, recounts memories of his life from earliest childhood in Vienna to his present situation confined in a state hospital on Wards Island. Greenberg recalls with special pleasure his early school days in the United States, writing "I was a reaper of hard fact and geographical bliss, a whole world of purity and history was given to me to take home and examine at my interest. It was an unusual thanks-given material that served as an unconscious guide to my spiritual labors." Other sources of childhood happiness were baseball games played in the streets and reading dime novels. He recalls also his family's sordid life in the tenements of the lower East Side of New York city, caught in "a dreary, cold-web sleeping-cave of rats and cabbage, sawdust floor – smelling sulphur fumes in an empty musical tomb." Later, there was the tedium of labor in a leather factory before "Sickness closed in with its careful teeth." Yet it was only during his enforced stays in a succession of charity hospitals that Samuel Greenberg at last possessed the time to read and to write poetry, producing in his few last years a remarkable and highly original body of work.

It is neither hyperbole nor exaggeration to say that Samuel Greenberg's poetry was without precedent in American writing. This solitary and untutored poet single-handedly invented American literary surrealism and, indeed, anticipated by some years the surrealist movement in Europe. Clearly, these poems will not be to everyone's taste. Ecstatic, excessive, dense, intense, held together by dream-logic and incantatory rhythms, they are likely to appeal primarily to readers receptive to the visionary and the mystical and responsive to what Aldous Huxley has named "verbal recklessness." By this is meant those poems written in an exalted state of uninhibited inspiration, poems drawing directly on the pre-conscious mind, the kind of poetry that breaks conventional dictionary meanings of words, together with their syntactical and logical order, releasing thereby their latent mysterious, magical power and opening, as Huxley says, "unsuspected windows onto the unknown." [3] Writing alone in the interstices "between historical life," Samuel Greenberg brought back from an inward elsewhere tokens of *convulsive beauty*. [4]

Conduct

By a peninsula, the painter sat and
sketched the uneven vally groves
The apostle. gave alms to the
Meek, The valcano burst
In fusive sulphor and hurled
Rocks and ore into the air,
Heaven's sudden change at
The drawing tempestrous
Darkening shade of Dense clouded Hues
The wanderer soon ahose
this spot of rest, they bore the
Chosen hero upon their shoulders
Whom they strangly admired - as,
The Beach tide Summer of people desired)

NOTES

---

[1] *The Poetry of Hart Crane: A Critical Study* by R.W.B. Lewis, Rahway, New Jersey: Princeton University Press, 1967, p. 181.

[2] "Poetic Matters" by Philip Lamantia in *Arsenal* No. 3, Spring 1976, p. 9.

[3] *Literature and Science* by Aldous Huxley, New Haven, Ct: Leete's Island Books, 1963, p. 35.

[4] The final sentence of André Breton's novel *Nadja* (1928) reads: "Beauty will be CONVULSIVE or will not be at all." Translation by Richard Howard, New York: Grove Press, 1960, p. 160.

ON THE DANGEROUS EDGE OF THINGS:
Weed: Adventures of a Dope Smuggler
by Jerry Kamstra
Peer Amid Press 2019
ISBN 978-1-7335481-0-6
312 pp. $20

This is, to be sure, a tale of adventure – a non-fiction, first-person account of moving a massive amount of marijuana from Mexico into the United States. The suspense and excitement attendant upon that enterprise, the cunning manoeuvres and minute particulars of the smuggler's trade as related by the author would be sufficient cause to recommend the book. But *Weed* is much more than that. It is equally a travelogue, with rich descriptions of the landscapes, towns, mountains and remote villages of Mexico, and a cultural commentary, both on Mexico and the United States. It is also a vivid portrayal of lives lived (in Robert Browning's phrase) "on the dangerous edge of things," lives pursued outside the law with all the implications and complications of that oblique stance.

Jerry Kamstra is a novelist (author of *The Frisco Kid* and other books) and knows how to structure and pace a story. *Weed* opens with a scene when the narrator is running the border at San Luis, Arizona with a load of 200 kilos of marijuana concealed in his car. At a U.S. custom's checkpoint his contraband cargo is detected by the inspectors and to evade arrest, he sprints back into Mexico, where he is shot at by the Mexican border guards, apprehended by them and then immediately returned to the custody of the U.S. authorities. He is subsequently tried in a

federal court, sentenced, and released on probation. Less than a year later – in violation of the terms of his probation – Kamstra decides to return to Mexico accompanied by his long-time smuggling partner (also a fugitive, actively sought by the FBI) in quest of the legendary marijuana fields of the Sierra Madre del Sur mountains. Ultimately, the two men reach the distant, fabled fields, purchasing there one ton of marijuana which they then arrange to import into the United States.

The events recounted in *Weed* take place in the mid 1960s – before, that is, the rise of large drug-trafficking cartels in Mexico – and the book was originally published by Harper & Row in 1974. Peer Amid Press has just issued this 45th Anniversary Edition, enhanced by an insightful introduction from the eloquent pen of Gerald Nicosia and a very useful condensed biography of the author written by the publisher, Daniel Yaryan. Also included in this handsome anniversary version of the book –

together with the black-and-white photographs taken by Gene Anthony that appeared in the original edition – are a number of fine pen-and-ink illustrations by artist Mat Fitzsimmons and decorations and vignettes by Kamstra himself.

As narrator of his own rakish tale, Kamstra comes across as modest and honest, candid about his gaffes and anxieties. He has a keen eye and a lively mind, is observant of people and places, sensitive to moods and vibes, receptive and reflective, and well-informed on a range of topics and contexts related to what he calls "the marijuana industry." His prose is by turns casual and lyrical, taut and digressive. The main narrative of the book is the journey undertaken by Kamstra and his Mexican-American partner Jesse deep into the mountains of Guerrero, their purchase there of a ton of quality marijuana and the complexities ensuing from their efforts to smuggle the load into the United States. The digressions are of several kinds – memories, explanations, anecdotes, analyses – usually pertinent to some immediate incident in the author's unfolding account of his venture.

Kamstra makes a number of incisive comments on subjects such as the consumerist-materialist mania he sees afflicting postwar American culture, the psychology of American law enforcement officials, the futility and the foreseeable contradictory consequences of government programs to stop drug trafficking, Mexican machismo, sexual repression in Mexico, and the varieties of oppression – overt and subtle – both south and north of the Mexican border. He is clearly knowledgeable about proper procedures for the cultivation of the marijuana plant, the potency and effects of diverse strains of marijuana, and well acquainted with the mythology and mystique surrounding the drug. Some of the author's most interesting observations concern the contrasting character and disposition of marijuana smugglers and marijuana dealers, and the differing mindsets and motivations to be found among the smugglers themselves, their varying goals and values. Kamstra is also a discerning observer of the nascent hippy phenomenon as it relates to Mexico and the marijuana trade, contrasting the hippies unfavourably to their predecessors the beats. (The hippies, in his experience, tend to be culturally insensitive and casually arrogant in their behaviour.)

Kamstra sketches lively portraits of the connections he makes in Mexico – the farmers and entrepreneurs, the *jefes* and peons – and provides fascinating details on the many dangers involved in purchasing and transporting marijuana, dangers that include soldiers, police, bandits and rival smugglers. Tactical problems arise constantly, careful reconnaissance must be made, contingency plans must be laid, security measures must be taken (including the hiring of *pistoleros* for protection) and incipient paranoia must be subdued. At the same time, vitally, continually, the invisible signs and signals must be heeded, and the subtle and elusive rhythm of an operation must be nurtured.

Though not uncritical of certain aspects of Mexican culture, Kamstra is never contemptuous or condescending in his views of the country and its inhabitants. Indeed, he feels a deep affinity with Mexico, is attracted by the landscapes, savours the food, and responds to the "sad, poignant, thunderous Mexico that exists behind the mountains, behind the silence, behind the stillness of the faces" of the Mexican people. His deepest esteem is for the Mexican poor, the Indians, the *campesinos,* or people of the fields. In their lives, in their communities, in their speech and gestures, he finds "honesty and grace and simple dignity," and "a profound strength," essential human qualities largely missing, he feels, from our technological culture.

Kamstra's bold outlaw ethos, his stubborn independence and his rapport with humble people have much in common with a writer who could be viewed as a kind of literary forebearer, Henri de Montfreid (1879-1974) author of *Adventures of a Red Sea Smuggler* (1935). More immediate literary connections can be seen with the writers of the Beat Generation, particularly Jack Kerouac. But Jerry Kamstra is very much his own man and *Weed* is a very individual book. The author's reflections on vanity, venality, fatality and integrity lend his personal adventure an enduring pertinence to the human adventure.